HOMETOWN VICTORY

A COACH'S STORY OF FOOTBALL, FATE, AND COMING HOME

KEANON LOWE

with JUSTIN SPIZMAN

FLATIRON
BOOKS
NEW YORK

HOMETOWN VICTORY. Copyright © 2022 by Keanon Lowe. All rights reserved. Printed in the United States of America. For information, address Flatiron Books, 120 Broadway, New York, NY 10271.

Designed by Donna Sinisgalli Noetzel

www.flatironbooks.com

The Library of Congress Cataloging-in-Publication Data is available upon request.

ISBN 978-1-250-80763-2 (hardcover)
ISBN 978-1-250-80764-9 (ebook)

Our books may be purchased in bulk for promotional, educational, or business use. Please contact your local bookseller or the Macmillan Corporate and Premium Sales Department at 1-800-221-7945, extension 5442, or by email at MacmillanSpecialMarkets@macmillan .com.

First Edition: 2022

10 9 8 7 6 5 4 3 2 1

In memory of Taylor Martinek

CONTENTS

Everyone you meet is fighting a
battle you know nothing about. Be kind.
Always.

—Robin Williams

HOMETOWN VICTORY

1

FRIDAY NIGHT LIGHTS

YOU'RE ALWAYS AUDITIONING
FOR SOMETHING

Y ou got the job." I pumped my fist in the air as I pressed the phone closer to my ear. "The committee was really impressed with you. I was really impressed with you. You would be a great fit as the next head football coach at Parkrose. Now, feel free to take some—"

I couldn't help myself. I interrupted Vice Principal Drake Shelton.

"Yes. Absolutely. I'll take it."

Drake let out a hearty laugh. "Okay, then. We're glad you want to be a Bronco! I'm excited to see what Coach Lowe can do! Why don't we set up a time for you to come back and meet the kids? Say Friday at noon? I can pull these kids out of lunch and we can set it up. I'll meet you at the auditorium. Oh, and you might want to start thinking about putting together a coaching staff, or at least try and get an assistant coach on board."

"Yes . . . absolutely. That sounds great. Friday. I will see you there."

My head buzzed. I couldn't help but be excited. I'd waited two weeks—which felt like months—for this phone call, not knowing if I would even be on a sideline this year. I was worried I'd botched the interview, opened up a bit too much.

It'd been a rocky year since my best friend and teammate died. When tragedy strikes, it often leaves you in a difficult headspace where, at times, life just doesn't make sense. I'd left my dream job as an up-and-coming young coach in the NFL to come back to my hometown and pick up the pieces. To be honest, I was struggling. Losing someone close to you is never easy, but it brought me back home and I was determined to find meaning in his tragedy. I was looking for something to help me move forward, but I didn't know what that "something" was. That is, until Parkrose High School came into the picture. They were looking for a new head football coach and I was looking for a purpose. Parkrose had its own set of challenges, making the coaching job about much more than just football. Located on the east side of Portland, Oregon, Parkrose was a school consistently affected by budget cuts and lack of resources. The majority of the student body came from hardworking, lower-income, and often broken families. The city of Portland is labeled as "the whitest city in America," but Parkrose didn't fit that bill. It was one of the few schools in the area that was a true melting pot of different ethnicities, cultures, and races. As a low-income district, the first programs to be affected when it came to school budgets were the sports programs. There was no tradition of success on the field or court. The Parkrose football program was the worst of them all, with a twenty-three-game losing streak dating back three seasons.

The thought of becoming the head coach at Parkrose excited me. More than just football, it was an opportunity to help a unique group of students that, quite frankly, needed it. The more I thought about it, the more it made sense. The job was an opportunity to pour my energy into kids that were in a similar situation as I was growing up. Like a lot of kids in our country, I came from a single-parent household. I never had much. My mom sacrificed a great deal to provide me, my brother, and my sister every opportunity, to give us the best chance at future success. Ultimately, she moved our family across town so I could attend Jesuit High School, a private college-preparatory school on the other side of Portland. Somehow my mom made it work, balancing multiple jobs to be able to pay the tuition. In return, I worked my butt off, on and off the field.

At Jesuit, there were unlimited resources. The teachers cared about you, and the coaches were invested, talented, and dedicated to the student's success. They did everything they could to get you to college and wouldn't let you slack academically. Parkrose was different. Not everyone could move away for a better opportunity like I did. These kids were here to stay, many of them fighting for a way to get out.

Football taught me my biggest life lessons. It was my vehicle. It's how I became an adult, how I grew into a young man. It's where I found my power and figured out firsthand that there truly is no greater feeling than being part of something that's bigger than yourself. I wanted to come in and give the students at Parkrose a similar opportunity, to show them that there are people out there who care about them. I wanted to be a role model and lifeline.

I'd said all this and more in the interview. They must have

been wondering why a former Oregon Duck and NFL coach would apply to a coaching ad that had been up for four months on Craigslist, but I hoped my passion would show through.

The school was on a 0–23 skid, and maybe I was delusional or just searching for some hope, but I believed I could turn it around in a year, no matter who the kids were. Success on a football field comes down to this: if you have a team that cares about each other, and a head coach that always puts his players first, anything is possible. I felt that if I could create a family within this team, then we would win. That's what's special about high school football—you get to play side by side with your best friends. It's a time in your life that you will remember forever, but you never get back. My high school teammates went from friends to family, and in some ways, I was here because I had just lost one of them.

I promised Drake that I would give the Parkrose kids what high school ball had given me.

More than the wins and losses, football is about the growth and the grind—the battle you fight within yourself and the lessons you take from them. When it's all said and done, our fondest memories aren't always the scoreboard, but the experience of working toward a common goal with your friends.

"Thanks again for the opportunity," I said. "I won't disappoint."

Drake paused for a second. "Son . . . there is only one way to go from here."

I put down the phone and smiled. I was about to embark on one of the greatest challenges of my entire life, but I was ready for it. I was just twenty-six years old, but I felt I had experienced a lot, learned a lot, and knew the path toward winning on and off the football field.

Even so, those around me didn't share my confidence and optimism. "Parkrose?" my mother had asked when I first applied for the position. "Why would you want to coach there?"

My mom, who was always my greatest supporter, hovered over me while I shoveled the last few bites of dinner into my mouth. It felt strange being back in Portland, after traveling the United States over the past five years. I'd played Division I football at the University of Oregon, and had coaching stops in Philadelphia and San Francisco on my résumé. Still, in many ways, it felt as if I had never left.

My mom had a point. Just last year I was standing next to Colin Kaepernick. It was a crazy run, being on the inside while watching him take a knee during the National Anthem. But now, as I sat back in my mom's small but warm home, I was ready to lead a program of my own. I looked up at my mom, locking on her always endearing and caring eyes.

"I don't know, Mom, but I have a good feeling about this. It feels right."

"But Keanon, those kids haven't won a football game in years. You sure you have enough patience for that?"

I loved my mom. I knew she was poking at me sarcastically, knowing far too well I was up for the challenge. I smiled at her.

"That's exactly why I want to give it a try. These kids need a mentor, someone they can look up to. Just think about what the coaches must have been like over the past couple seasons. You don't lose every game because of a bunch of high-schoolers. Coaches who don't give a damn are the reason you lose every game. I don't know, Mom . . . it just feels like something I need to do."

I remembered going to local high school football games

growing up and watching Parkrose get absolutely destroyed week after week. For the last twenty years, Parkrose was the laughingstock of Portland-area high school football. Not much had changed. When I applied to be the next football coach, Parkrose was the same struggling program I remembered as a kid.

The other teams didn't even take their games against Parkrose seriously. It was a get-right game, one you could easily overlook on the schedule because you knew it would be a layup. When it came to football, Parkrose was a joke. But I planned to change that. I wanted to win. No matter where I was, I demanded greatness and always played to win. Call it the athlete in me, but I didn't accept second place all that well.

"Alright, Keanon." She smiled. "Show them why you're the guy."

Even though my mom had a way of challenging me, she always made it known how much she cared. Growing up with a single mother will do that to you. She was firm, but never held back her love for us. It wasn't easy to play the role of both a mother and a father to three children, but Mom always made it work. She did her best to ensure we had enough. My mom always left it all on the field.

I spent the next few days preparing to meet the kids: pulling up old playbooks, reviewing film of the Parkrose kids playing ball the past two seasons, and working on a preliminary list of the drills we'd run during practice. But I still hadn't found an assistant coach to help me out.

I had a lot of football friends in the Portland area, and I called damn near every single one of them. I got the same response from most:

"Parkrose? Like the Parkrose that hadn't won a game since the nineties?"

"Come on, Keanon . . . you really took a job with those guys?"

"You know you're my boy, but I can't do that."

"Man, I got enough stuff going on in my life, you don't know what you're getting yourself into."

Who could blame them? Parkrose did stink, ever since we were little. As I worked my way through my cell phone and called nearly every one of my former teammates still in Portland, I finally arrived at Brian Jackson. B-Jax, as we called him at Oregon, was a bone-shattering defensive back from Hoover, Alabama, who loved to hit. He was a no-nonsense baller, and there were many practices where I lined up against him on offense. Way too many of these plays ended up with me and him scuffling, pushing, and jawing in the middle of the field. Coach Chip Kelly, or whoever was closest to us, would run over and have to break it up. But we had a mutual respect for one another and were always cool off the field.

Figuring he might be willing to give it a shot and with my options dwindling, I gave him a call. By some miracle, he was willing to hear me out past the point where I told him about the open coaching position at Parkrose. We spoke about the school and its lack of support and unique demographics. I tried my best to explain to him, as the committee explained to me, that Parkrose didn't have a bunch of athletes, high-quality facilities, or resources at all. It would be an uphill battle, but I was willing to fight it. B-Jax, maybe just to help a brother out, agreed to join my staff. One became two.

Friday came, and I grabbed my computer bag, double-checked my tie in the mirror near the door, and headed out for my new job. Parkrose was exactly as I remembered it, as if frozen in time. The district hadn't put much time or energy into updating the outdated building. You could see a few haphazardly applied coats of paint on the outside of the building, but it was like putting lipstick on a pig more than anything else.

After parking my car, I walked into the beaten-down building, looking for signs to the administrator's office. When I found out, I opened the door and was greeted by an elderly woman with oversized glasses and a voluminously coiffed head of hair. "Hey, honey . . . you here for the coaching gig?"

"Yes, ma'am. I am. My name is Keanon Lowe, and I am scheduled to meet with the athletic director, Daunte Gouge."

"Okay, sweetie. Have a seat. I will let him know you are here."

She then picked up the phone, and I could hear her speak with Daunte. A few minutes later, a door behind her opened and a skinny, red-haired man wearing sweats and a zip-up hoodie with the Parkrose emblem walked through.

"That must be my man Coach Lowe!" Daunte said. "Hey, bud . . . good to have you here. Come on in, everyone is waiting to meet you."

We walked to the front of the auditorium where B-Jax and Vice Principal Drake Shelton were waiting. Everyone introduced themselves, and Daunte turned to me.

"You ready, son? This is going to be interesting. We told all the kids on the team last year that wanted to play again to meet in the auditorium at twelve to get to know the new head coach. No one told them who it would be, so they are in for a surprise.

I went ahead and put together a little video introduction, I hope you don't mind. It's mostly your highlight reel from Oregon, but I wanted to get the kids hyped up for the season."

I stopped dead in my tracks.

"Wait . . . highlight reel? Daunte . . . that's really not my thing. I just wanted to say what's up, get to know the kids, shake their hands, you know, that sort of thing. I'd really prefer if you . . ."

Daunte looked at me and slapped me on the back in an endearing sort of way. "Look, Keanon. These kids have been getting their asses kicked every single game for the last three seasons. Let's try and give them something to be excited about."

B-Jax loved it and started poking and prodding me. "Man, Lowe . . . I don't know how they could put all those highlights in just a two-minute video," he laughed. "This is going to be a tough one."

We walked into the auditorium and took our spots right in front of the stage. Looking around the auditorium, I noticed the same theme here as I did throughout the rest of the school. It was beaten up, had seen better days, and was in desperate need of an update. The auditorium had maybe five hundred seats in it, and there were two large doors at the top that fed into the arena-like structure. The lights were dimmed in anticipation of my Hollywood debut. Heat crept into my cheeks as I flushed. Sure, I was the head coach, but this job wasn't about me.

We heard the bell ring, signaling the lunch hour, and a bunch of young men started to trickle in through the two doors. It was a strange experience, seeing my team walk through the doors. As one of the few truly diverse schools in Portland, there were students from many different races and cultures walking the halls: Polynesian, Asian, Mexican, Black, and white students filled the auditorium in equal numbers. Some of the kids looked like prototypical football archetypes, while others looked like they were lost and had wandered into the wrong room.

From that first glance, I started to mentally place them in positions on the field. There was my defensive line, my corners, my wide receivers, maybe even my QB. I had to pinch myself, still unsure if this were real. Almost fifty kids later, Daunte signaled to someone at the top of the auditorium. The lights went dark, and a grainy old YouTube video appeared on the projector screen at the front. Totally embarrassed, and somewhat shocked, I held my head down in shame, as if we were about to watch a blooper reel instead of a highlight reel.

"He played at the University of Oregon," Daunte said, doing his best imitation of a boxing ring announcer. "He coached in the NFL for the Eagles and the 49ers. Please meet your new coach— Keanon Lowe!"

Some of the players were clearly impressed, but most couldn't have cared less. But I didn't want to take away Daunte's moment. He clearly cared deeply for the kids and was giddy about my hiring. After suffering through the three-minute video, the lights came up and Daunte signaled for me to address the team.

I quickly surveyed the now well-lit room, looking at the fifty young men, each with different stories, experiences, backgrounds, and needs.

"Thanks for the intro, Mr. Gouge. I appreciate that." I took a beat, trying to figure out how best to connect. As I looked around, I noticed many of the kids were wearing hats, hoodies, and headphones covering their ears. "Before we start, I want everyone in the room to pull back your hoodies, take off your earphones, put away your cell phones. I will always show you respect, and I appreciate you doing the same with me. So, take them off and we can get started."

The kids paused, looked at me, unsure what to do. After a few seconds they all started motioning to each other and removing their hats, hoodies, and headphones.

"Thanks, guys. It is great to meet you. I really am excited . . ." As the words came out of my mouth, B-Jax calmly put his hand on my back. I looked behind me just in time to see him take three steps forward and point his hand in the area of three young men in the stands who'd ignored my direction.

"Hey . . . hey . . . you three. Coach K said to take off your hoodies. You need to listen to him and respect his requests of you."

B-Jax then stepped back and whispered into my ear, "All yours, Coach."

We had to make it clear to these young men that we were the coaches, and they were the players. While there would be a level of mutual respect between the two of us, we weren't going to take one ounce of attitude from anyone. These kids had had very little discipline or direction leading up to this point, and if we wanted to come together as a team, this small gesture was crucial.

I stood tall and spoke to my guys for the first time. "From this point forward, you and me are family. I can't tell you how excited I am to be standing here as your new head coach. I know we just met, and there will be time for us to build that trust, but from this day forward we're family and you can ask me for anything. All I need from you is your respect and you will get mine in return. I know we haven't won a game in a while, and I can tell you, from firsthand experience, that I don't like losing any more than you do. I am here to teach you how to win."

Everyone paid attention now. They were silent. All eyes on me. Locked in to every word that came out of my mouth. They'd never heard one of their coaches sound like a coach. They could tell I was serious.

"As your coaches, it is our job to come up with the plan. It is our job to help you get stronger, faster, and become better football players. As a player it is your job to follow through with the plan we lay out. And make no mistake about it, fellas, we have a plan. I don't care what happened last season or what's gone on in the past around here. Everyone has a clean slate and a fresh start. I have goose bumps right now because I can feel it." I lifted up my arm and looked into their faces. "I can feel that this is the start of something special."

Not a single kid in that room had ever won a game before, but in that short moment in the auditorium we all felt something take over the room that hadn't been at Parkrose for a long time: belief. A belief that we might have a chance to take the field together and perform. That we could battle together and come out stronger than before. And maybe, just maybe, a belief that we could win.

"Now, before you leave, Coach Jackson and I would like the chance to shake everyone's hand and meet all you guys. We'll be up here."

It took the kids a minute, but they rose, one by one, and started to make their way down the auditorium steps. Every kid in that auditorium lined up single file. They each shook my hand, then B-Jax's. Some of the kids had a firm handshake and made good eye contact with us. Others—not so much. Some of the kids were nervous and clammy. Some of the kids didn't even know how to properly shake an adult's hand, so Brian and I taught them.

"No, no, like this, like this." We took the time for every single one of them.

We encouraged the kids who came up and introduced themselves in feeble and soft voices: "Speak up, man. It's all good."

Toward the end of the line stood one of the kids who hadn't initially taken off his hoodie. He looked like a football player. He was built, tall, muscular, and clearly an athlete. As he walked up to me, he quickly apologized for keeping his hoodie on. That was a good start.

"No problem, man," I said. "Thanks for taking it off. I appreciate that."

He looked me in the eye, offering a firm handshake.

"My name is Tre Singleton."

"Well, Tre, it's nice to meet you. You ready to play some football?"

He smiled a million-dollar smile.

"You bet, Coach."

As he walked past us, I looked at Brian with a sense of relief.

"We got ourselves some football players here." B-Jax and I started going back and forth about the kids and positions, and I hardly noticed Daunte circle around us until he whispered in my ear.

"You see this last kid walking down the stairs?"

We turned and saw a young man walking down the stairs with Vice Principal Drake Shelton. Even from a distance in the dim auditorium, I could tell he was made to be an athlete.

"Well, that's Jay'Veontae Hudson, but everyone calls him Jay Jay. He didn't come out and play last season. He played as a freshman but got into it with the coach and ended up quitting the team. Well, he's back. I think this year, he wants to give it another go. And this kid can play, Coach. Hands down the best athlete on campus. He has a bright future in football if he decides to apply himself."

"Well, that's good news because he looks like an NFL receiver already."

Jay Jay walked up to me, with the assistant principal by his side, and shook my hand. "Hey bud, I'm Coach Lowe. It's good to meet you. You ready for a fresh start?"

Sensing that things would be different this time around, Jay Jay's eyes lit up at my warm welcome.

"Let's ball, Coach."

2

LOSING A BROTHER

THERE'S A THREAT TO YOUR SUCCESS
AROUND EVERY CORNER

Still at the meet and greet, Drake was covering the room with me. "I want to introduce you to someone," Vice Principal Drake Shelton said as he gestured to one of the students to come talk to us. "He's going to be a good player for you if you can keep him in line." As the young man approached, Drake said, "Kimball—come say hello to your new football coach."

Kimball Moeaki walked over slowly, avoiding eye contact with me at all costs. As I surveyed him, the football coach in me immediately started to think about the possibilities. He stood at an intimidating six feet tall and had to be over two hundred and twenty-five pounds. He had stood out in the auditorium, and it was refreshing to get an official introduction from Drake. I reached out my hand.

"Kimball, how you doin', bro? Good to see you."

"Hey, Mr. Shelton. Hey, Coach Lowe, I'm doing good." He responded quietly but with a strong handshake. For as big and intimidating as he looked, his soft-spoken nature took me by surprise.

Drake gave me a mischievous look. "His mom calls him Kimball. But around school they call him Polo."

Kimball laughed under his breath and looked toward the ground.

Drake went on, "When he's going to class and doing the right thing, he's Kimball. But when he's in my office and not taking care of business, he's Polo."

We all let out a laugh while Drake put his hand on Kimball's broad shoulder. Drake looked at him, half joking, half serious. "We don't like to see Polo, do we?"

Kimball smiled and shook his head side to side. "You right, Shelton. You right."

Kimball and I talked a bit more. That was precisely why I was at school—to meet the kids. I decided to start showing up even when we didn't have practice, dropping into the kids' classes, showing up at lunchtime, and even chatting them up after the bell rang. It seemed like important work to be present, to show this group of outsiders that I would be a constant in their lives. If nothing else, I would make sure they knew me as one person they could count on.

Like most students at Parkrose, Kimball came from humble beginnings. He came from a proud, hardworking Polynesian family. His mother works as a caregiver. His father owned and operated the family business, a concrete company. Kimball, or Polo, depending on the day, was the youngest of six siblings: four older brothers and an older sister. His island roots led him to play rugby as a kid, but he eventually tried his luck at football early in his high school career. Since the requisite skill set for the two sports are so closely related, he excelled at both.

"Well, what sport do you like better?" I asked, teasing him.

"Rugby," he fired back. "We don't need pads in rugby!"

The kid had heart and was built like a brick house. He was quiet but had a cool confidence that put those around him at ease.

Meeting the kids made everything start to feel real. This was going to happen. I had my first head coaching job, and there was a lot of work to do. As head coach, it was my job to guide this team through the ups and downs, the wins and losses, in order to build something bigger than just each individual player. Perhaps that is what makes the opportunity to be a head coach so special—you get to be the avenue for change.

I had wanted to be a coach for as long as I could remember. As my playing career wound down, and I came to terms with the fact that I wouldn't be playing ball for the rest of my life, I still felt football was my calling. There was always something about it: the comradery, the competition, the blood, sweat, and tears. Football, as a sport, had it all. Football, as a metaphor for life, made perfect sense to me.

Leading up to Parkrose, I had spent time coaching in the NFL with the Eagles and 49ers. This experience helped shape me into who I was when I walked into that auditorium, but not for the reason many would think. Sure, it was the Big Leagues—it was remarkable to see athletes and coaches perform at the highest level, but what really helped me grow as a man was the moment during my time with the NFL that transcended football. I was coaching with the 49ers over the course of the 2016 season when Colin Kaepernick took a knee. A time when football meant more than just the game. I am a product of every team I've played on, every one of the athletes I coached, and every game we won and lost on the gridiron. But that season sticks out. It shaped my life in a way that I will never forget.

Colin and I became close, talking about football, the paths that had led us to the game, and race as I helped him rehab from his shoulder injury. The struggles that Colin was taking a stand against were the same struggles these kids at Parkrose had to deal with day in and day out and would no doubt continue to face for the rest of their lives.

I knew something of what they'd been through. I experienced racism and bigotry growing up. But let's be honest, if you're a person of color, you can probably recall any number of moments when you were judged because of the color of your skin. I am mixed race—I was too "black" for white people and too "white" for Black people. But sports had always bridged the gap for me, and my talents likely gave me a path to acceptance I might not have had otherwise. People loved a winning team more than they disliked many of us for having a different skin color. Many of my Black teammates recognized that they were accepted because they could run fast, hit hard, or catch a football. But as team-mates, we were all equal in the locker room and in the huddle, and that was no clearer than when the players on the 49ers and Coach Chip Kelly rallied around Colin and supported his right to kneel. Maybe that is part of what makes sports so special. A group of people from different walks of life can come together and trust and love one another because they share a common interest. Acceptance is not based on skin color, but on your commitment to giving your all and being there for your teammates on the field. In your pursuit of victory, you shed the barriers of race and the only color that matters is the one on your uniform. I wanted to bring that to the Parkrose kids.

During my first few days on the job, I shadowed Drake around school. Each day was a learning opportunity and a chance to start a relationship with one of my new players. I was calculated in my approach. I'd show up at noon each day during lunchtime, the best part of any high-schooler's day. These kids needed to get to know me before I demanded anything of them, which became clearer each time I learned more about the Parkrose struggle from Drake.

"You know why I think you'll do a great job here, K-Lowe?" Drake asked. We stood side by side on the outside edges of the cafeteria.

Not sure how to answer, I stood there with my arms crossed and remained silent as the students buzzed around us. I figured the question was rhetorical.

"You see our students?" he said, motioning to the hundreds of kids that sat at the lunch tables in front of us. Each table had a different style, vibe, and clique. Some kids were laughing and joking, others yelling and arguing. The personality of the student body was on full display.

"You're going to do a great job here . . . because our students look like you."

I stood there with a half smile and nodded in agreement.

"You have to understand, that's a big deal. Especially to your football boys. Your guys don't have many real-life examples of young men of color, doing good things with their lives. That's powerful, man."

Drake was twenty years into his career as an educator, a veteran when it came to leading and helping kids through the challenges of life and high school. He was hired as vice principal three years before I got there, and understood these kids better than anyone, in part because as a Black man he could connect in a way other teachers and administrators could not. At Parkrose, he made it clear, that would be my advantage as well. Though his career must have included many obstacles, he set an example of how far you can go if you always put the kids first. When Drake Shelton spoke, I listened.

"You're going to give them someone to look up to. They need someone like you. They need to see what is possible."

Listening to Drake confirmed my belief that I was exactly where I was supposed to be. Maybe he was just building his young football coach up. Or maybe he actually believed in what I brought to the table. It was probably a mix of both, but it didn't matter much in the moment. With someone like Drake Shelton behind me, I felt like I couldn't fail.

The bell rang and the students methodically got up from the lunch tables and returned to class, leaving behind a mess of plastic wrappers, paper bags, and lunch trays. After the students cleared out the cafeteria, Shelton began to walk around and pick up the hurricane left in their wake. Even as the vice principal, he wasn't scared to do the dirty work. I caught on quick and followed suit. As we walked from table to table picking up the trash, we kept talking about the students. Drake was an encyclopedia of information and never hesitated to share his opinion on the direction of the football program. He had a background in coaching ball, and wasn't shy to tell you about it.

"Coach, I tell you what. This group of guys you have this year are talented." Like me, he was an optimist. "You have the pieces to make it work, you just have to figure out a way to get these boys to buy in."

"Let me guess, easier said than done?" I jokingly replied.

He laughed, sensing the sarcasm in my voice. "Nothing's easy around here, Coach." Drake was in charge of all disciplinary issues at the school so if anyone knew the struggle of the student body, he did. "There's a couple guys that can be real players for you," he said. "Just make sure you don't let one of the bad eggs spoil the bunch."

"Bad egg?" My ears perked up with curiosity.

"Damn right, bad egg," he laughed as we continued to hover from table to table picking up the garbage. "His name's RJ. The kid is everything you want on the football field, in between the lines, but everywhere else," he warned me, "let's just say . . . he struggles."

"Well, what kind of struggle are we talking about?" I asked.

Drake stopped picking up the plastic wrappers and looked me in my face.

"He's the type of kid we call *fair-weather*. That's not an uncommon theme around here. When things are good, the kid is great. He's a joy to be around. Those are the times when he has no problems whatsoever." He paused. "But when things are bad, you better watch out. When things are bad, they are *really* bad.

"But he's got a chance," he added. "He's a good kid, just a little lost."

Out of all the kids in the program, Drake singled out RJ Artis. It must have been for good reason. Still, I was eager for the challenge.

"Can I meet him?" I blurted out, without thinking.

"Right now?" Drake asked.

"Yeah, let's do it. Can we pull him from class for a few minutes?"

He nodded in agreement. "I like the way you think. Follow me."

We finished cleaning the last table and went to his office to look up the room number RJ was in. Drake gestured to the chair in front of the desk as he sat down at his computer.

"Make yourself comfortable. This should only take a second."

"Thanks." I sat down and fired away. "So what else can you tell me about RJ?"

Drake took his hands off the keyboard and leaned back in his chair. "Where should I start? Well, let's just say RJ is one of those kids that does things his own way. Whether it's school or football, he calls his own shots. This will be his senior year coming up. He's come a long way since we first got him as a freshman, but in all honesty, we're running out of time. I worry about kids like him when they leave high school." The tone in his voice softened. There was no more sarcasm in the conversation, he was being real.

"He's had a rough go at it. Dealt some tough cards, Coach. Single mom, real rough part of town and bad living situation. He's been through it his entire life, so you can't blame the kid."

I could tell Mr. Shelton had a soft spot for RJ. He finished pulling up his class schedule on the computer before we took to the hallways. "Alright got it, room 206, English class."

As we walked, the reality of my new job continued to sink in. The longer I was there and the more I learned about these students, the more attached I became. The more personal it all felt. Parkrose wasn't the dilapidated and abandoned school so many outsiders presumed it to be. Rather, it was a place of great energy, effort, diversity, and love. There was just something missing.

We walked up to room 206 and Mr. Shelton gently knocked, opened the door, and stuck his head in, motioning toward RJ to step in the hallway with him.

RJ stood. He was my height, five foot nine, with copper-colored skin and a head of messy curls. In my eyes, he looked like a star wide receiver, and from what Mr. Shelton said, he had the bravado to match.

As soon as he stepped out of the classroom, he recognized me.

"Ayy, what's up, Coach," RJ said. We shook hands. He had a tough aura about him, but I was determined.

"Not much, not much. Just checking in, bro," I responded. "How you been, I heard a lot about you."

He looked at Drake and nudged him with his elbow. "Hopefully it was all good things."

"You know it!" Drake playfully shot back at him. "I didn't want to scare Coach Lowe off too soon, he just got here!"

We shared a collective laugh. I could tell Drake and RJ had a good relationship. The kind of relationship that's been years in the making. As we continued to make small talk, I could tell RJ was being cautious with me, making sure he kept a straight face with minimal emotion. He was confident in himself and clearly wasn't worried about striking up a friendship with his new coach. Although he wasn't openly excited to talk to me, he was still listening and interested in what I was saying. He was wary, and I don't blame him. Trust is earned, not given. I would have to prove myself and continue to show up for him.

"I'm going to count on you this off-season," I said. "When we get started I'm going to need you to be a leader."

He responded with all I needed to hear: "Yes, Coach. I got you."

We shook hands and RJ returned to class. He was respectful and ultimately excited to have a coach that could finally teach him football, although he did his best not to show it. RJ would be my first Parkrose coaching challenge, and while I'd faced many obstacles on the football field, I'd never quite faced one like this.

RJ had all the skills to excel on the field but lacked the tools a young person needs to combat the inevitable adversities that life brings. He loved football, but constantly struggled to deal with the ups and downs of the sport. Through much of his life, he struggled with anger and disciplinary issues. People who knew RJ all had the same thing to say about him: he had great potential on and off the field but needed someone to press him forward to achieve all he could in both areas. Although I appreciated the background on these kids, I made it a point to never let their reputations influence my goals and path for them. Everyone would get a fresh start, including RJ.

If I was going to ask these kids to go to battle with me, they had to know I would always be by their side. In just a few months I would start demanding a lot from them, and it made sense to show them I would be there every step of the way. I didn't yet know each kid's full story, but it seemed like so few of them had people who truly dedicated themselves to their growth and success. I wanted to be that person.

One day after school, I took a walk outside to the equipment shed to take inventory. As I approached the shed, in the distance I saw a young man on the field maneuvering through orange agile cones. From over a hundred yards away I could tell this kid was lightning quick. He cut and chopped his way through and around those cones like he was skating on ice. But the most impressive thing about him wasn't the footwork, it was the fact that this young man was outside after school, working out by himself. You can tell the most about someone's character by how they carry themselves when no one's looking. I had to go see who this kid was, so I skipped the equipment shed and beelined to the field.

"What's goin' on, man, I'm Coach Lowe," I said as I walked up to him. I recognized his face from that first introduction in the auditorium.

"What's good, Coach? Just getting my work in."

"Remind me of your name again? I know we met a couple weeks ago." I extended my fist for a greeting. He reached out and dapped me up.

"Taydrian Jackson."

Taydrian was a small but well-put-together kid. He wasn't the most physically imposing player, but by the looks of it he had to be the quickest kid we had.

"Good to see you again, Tay. Tell me something about yourself, and I'll leave you alone so you can get back to work. What grade you in? What position do you play?" I asked.

"No worries, Coach. I'll be a junior next season. And next year I want to play running back. I played running back my whole life except last year."

"What did they have you playing last year?"

Taydrian shook his head. "They didn't have a QB for the varsity team so they put me back there."

"Quarterback?" I exclaimed. "You don't move around those cones like a quarterback!" He was a little small in stature to be a QB, even for a high-schooler.

"Yeah, Coach." I could hear the disappointment in his voice.

"It wasn't very fun for me. I was back there running for my life every Friday night."

"Well, Tay, let's get you back to your roots then," I affirmed. "You just keep doing exactly what you're doing. You're my running back, so get ready to get in the end zone."

"Yessir! I'll be ready!" he replied, confidently and quickly.

Taydrian was clearly self-motivated. The best thing I could do for a kid like that is do my part to set him up for success and then get out of his way.

As the weeks went on and I continued to walk the grounds, I grew more attached to this place. With every student athlete I met, I became more inspired to do my part and not let them down. It seemed every single one of these kids had a complicated backstory and a little bit more beneath the surface. While different in many ways, football connected us. A bunch of hash marks, not-so-green grass, and a pigskin were the common denominators between me and each of these young men. I was hungry to help these boys, starting with helping them get ready for their first football win.

To get things moving, Coach B-Jax and I decided to organize workouts in the weight room after school. Even though they were targeted toward the players at the initial meeting, I labeled them as "open workouts" in hopes of welcoming anyone that wanted to play football. Students at Parkrose quit when things got tough, and it was unfortunately embedded within the culture of the school, especially in the athletic programs. It was important not to demand anything of the kids yet, not until I gained their trust.

"What do you think about three days a week?" I asked B-Jax, knowing he was never shy to share his opinion.

"Well, what are you trying to accomplish?" he asked after a beat.

That was a good question. When it came to strength training B-Jax was my guy. He doubled as a certified trainer when he wasn't coaching with me. After his playing days at the University of Oregon, he took his passion for weight lifting and made it a profession. He could draw up a weight lifting plan at the drop of a hat.

"Honestly, here's how I see it. I want to have something after school that gives the guys a chance to get to know us. But if we make it mandatory, I'm afraid we'll scare most of them off. We have to show them we're committed to them. We can talk about it all we want, but if we want these boys to eventually commit to us, we have to prove we'll do it first."

B-Jax agreed. "Actions speak louder than words."

If I was going to ask them to run through a brick wall for me, and that was my intention, they had to know I would be waiting for them on the other side. But we had a ways to go before we got to that point.

We'd had fifty kids at the first meeting in the auditorium, so I figured we'd have a packed house for our first weight room workout. B-Jax and I put in a lot of time and energy planning the logistics, ensuring we laid out a thoughtful and organized strength program for the kids. We settled on three days a week. The trick was making it easy enough to ensure we didn't scare them off, yet challenging enough to keep their interest.

During my lunchtime visits I passed the message along to my players, making sure I verbally reminded them the date and time of our optional workouts. I made PARKROSE FOOTBALL flyers and put them up around the school. The word got out, the flyers were hung, and the weight lifting program was set. I was ready to get my first real look at what these guys could do. The night before, I envisioned my first team activity as a head coach. I planned the message I might deliver and the way I would encourage the boys. I was like a kid on Christmas Eve, I could hardly contain my excitement. *What if all fifty kids show up?* I thought, right before shutting my eyes to sleep. The weight room wasn't quite big enough for fifty but I would cross that bridge when I got there.

I was juiced as the bell rang, signaling the end of school and beginning of the first after-school workouts. B-Jax and I were standing near the door to the weight room, a dilapidated area at the top of the old gym. The weights were outdated, chipped, and rusty. Many of the machines looked as if they were produced in some sort of medieval torture chamber. But we were surrounded by tons of steel, and that was all we needed to get these kids moving in the right direction.

The clock inched toward 3:45 P.M., the scheduled start of the workout. Excited and ready to get this thing going, I counted under my breath, "One . . . two . . . three . . . four . . . five . . ." as I walked into the weight room.

Five kids stood in front of me. I had expecting well over thirty at the first workout. I looked around in disbelief.

"This is it?" B-Jax said with a confused look on his face.

We could barely field a starting basketball team. My excitement immediately deflated. I'd spent the last few weeks showing up and putting in the time to get to know the guys. Leading up to that day, every kid I told about the open workout responded with the same thing: "I'll be there, Coach!"

That moment was a major reality check. Maybe this thing wasn't going to be as smooth as I anticipated, I thought to myself.

I'd soon learn that, at Parkrose, we didn't have *football players*. We had kids that played football. There's a big difference. Our kids didn't grow up playing in the street or watching football every Sunday like many young people that are obsessed with the game. At Parkrose, most kids looked at football as simply something to do in their spare time if convenient.

I took a beat to feel sorry for myself but quickly snapped back into it, determined to make the best of the situation. We had to focus on the positives, something we often had to do just to mentally survive Parkrose. At the end of the day there were still five players that made the choice to show up. It was a far cry from fifty, but five was a start.

Among the five players who showed up, I spotted Tre Singleton, RJ Artis, and Taydrian Jackson. Three kids that flat-out loved ball. With the right dose of attention and encouragement, these kids could be the anchor of our team.

We hit the ground running with the kids that made the choice to show that day. I decided to take everything in stride and not worry about who *wasn't* there and instead put all my energy and efforts into who *was* there. It was crucial to make sure that whoever did show up, and whoever did decide to commit, would get my full attention. It was February, and the season was months away. There would be time to improve attendance.

Over the first two months, I continued to show up and prove my loyalty. Three times a week at 3:45 P.M., I came to the weight room prepared with a new workout plan and focus for the day. On a good day, we would have as many as eight kids. On a bad day, the workout group dwindled to two. I was doing everything I could to build these kids up from scratch, from the ground level, but it was draining. Often, after a workout, I would drive home defeated, questioning myself and my strategy. I did my best to stay positive, but in reality, it wasn't looking good.

Getting my guys to come work out with me was a vicious cycle. A kid would show up for three days in a row, and then not for another three weeks. Others would show up and do a workout, realize it was more difficult than expected, and then never show again. Only a few really stuck with it and wanted to be a part of building a program. Sure, there were fifty kids that first day, but we were building the program from scratch. Brick by brick. Kid by kid.

After a few weeks, things weren't looking any better. The administrators and teachers informed me that participation in sports was a big problem with the kids at Parkrose. They quit easily. If things didn't go right the first time for them, then they'd just drop it. Often they'd quit all their sports teams. Many students skipped classes or didn't show up for school at all. Bucking that trend wouldn't be easy. I'd have to build something that would matter to them, something they wanted to show up for, maybe even for the first time in their lives.

At most schools, you had players of all ages ready to jump at the chance to play ball. At our school, we had a grand total of five. But you had to start somewhere, and after a couple months I learned to embrace it. In a place where positive energy was rare and excuses rampant, I was fighting against an entire culture. Our workouts fell short of my expectations but still offered some great insight and opportunity to learn about some of the kids, especially RJ and Tre.

These two young men in particular had plenty of ups and downs. They often struggled with behavioral challenges, discipline, and putting forth effort into something constructive. None of that mattered to me. You could see, clear as day, the potential these young dudes had. As much as B-Jax and I banged on them to push, push, push, we also wanted to get to know them as kids outside of football.

While I didn't know what these kids knew about me or my past as a football player and coach, it wasn't hard for them to find out. In many ways, they couldn't believe it. RJ would always playfully remind me, "Yo, Coach K . . . what did you do to get kicked out of the NFL and have to coach us? You were coaching Kap last fall and now you're at Parkrose. You know we haven't won a game in three years, right?" All jokes aside, it was a fair question. I let them take their playful shots, but it struck me as a sad situation that they were so down on themselves and lacked such confidence that they couldn't even consider why anyone would want to coach them.

As we closed one workout, I decided to call in the kids.

"Hey guys . . . there's that pizza restaurant around the corner. Let's call it early today and go eat. Coach K is buying. Get cleaned up and meet me there in twenty."

The small group of players looked at each other, realizing this was their opportunity to avoid the next fifteen minutes of torturous burnouts, and were out of there as quick as the words came from my mouth.

B-Jax and I were left to rack the weights and close down the workout room. He looked at me, somewhat unsure about going out with the players, and said, "You sure about this, Coach?" I didn't hesitate. "Yeah, why not? We're family. Besides, these boys earned it. It would be good to spend some time with them outside of the weight room."

Round Table Pizza was just a block away from Parkrose.

I walked over with B-Jax, and as we opened the restaurant door, we could see the boys had already gotten a table and were ordering drinks. We sat, and I ordered three large pizzas and some wings for the table.

"Look guys . . . we are a family," I said. "It is important we spend time together outside of the gym as well. This isn't just about getting your bodies strong and prepared for the season. It's also about trusting one another and realizing we're all in this thing together." Tre, marinating in my comments, looked up from his giant glass of soda.

"I don't mean this to be rude, Coach, but you never did answer RJ's question. Why did you leave the NFL? Why are you here with us, at Parkrose?"

It was a fair question. One I had thought about and clearly knew the answer.

"Well, I came back because of one of my old teammates. His name is Taylor Martinek. All of us on his team called him T-Mart. I met Taylor my freshman year of high school, a lot like how you guys met. We were together not too far from here, at Jesuit."

The kids began to boo, as Jesuit was a state powerhouse and local private school.

"I know, I know. I wasn't from around there, so I didn't really know anyone. We had just moved across the city so I could go play ball there. My goal was to play college football, so my mom moved us across the river so I would have a better shot. A lot of those kids from Jesuit High School came from Catholic elementary and middle schools from all over. And I came from a public school. I was the new kid, in more ways than one.

"We met at the football camp and became friends from the jump. He lived close to the school, a five-minute walk. So a lot of guys on the freshmen football team were coming from the other side of the city. Taylor opened his house to us to sleep over, so we didn't have to wake up early and travel across town. He was a good dude. That's just who he was, ever since that freshmen football camp, we were best friends. All through high school, we'd hang after practice, chase girls, go to parties, movies. You know, those high school things. We had a lot in common, but the biggest thing was our love for the game. That's what we did and who we were."

Tre cut me off.

"What position did he play?"

I responded with pride, "Middle linebacker, like you. The dude was a savage on the field, First-Team All-State. Under those Friday night lights, you couldn't touch us.

"When he was a senior in high school," I continued, "he hurt his shoulder. His labrum was torn but he passed on the surgery and decided to finish the year and get it fixed after the season . . . That's when things really started to change for him. That was the first time he was exposed to painkillers."

The pit in my stomach started to swell up again just thinking about it. Just two years ago, T-Mart was here. Both of us, twenty-four-year-old college graduates with our whole lives ahead.

"After high school, I played for the Ducks and Taylor went on to play at Portland State once he healed up. We stayed in touch and spoke every couple days, but Taylor suffered a few more injuries over the course of the next couple years. More injuries meant more surgery, and with those surgeries meant more pills. And things went from bad to worse. The injuries piled up and Taylor had to quit playing ball altogether. It crushed him.

"Having something you love get taken away from you, especially when it's out of your control, is tough. That's when he started to become addicted to the pills. He became like a lot of people in our country who get prescribed opioids to stop the pain, but then, all of a sudden, need them just to get through the day. It's a scary thought, a pill designed to help you, but ultimately can harm you if you're not careful."

As I talked, I hardly even noticed the waitress had returned with another waiter. They were holding three extra-large pizzas and a bucket of wings. They placed them throughout the table, and you didn't have to tell these kids to go ahead and start. They dove right in, grabbing the food as if they hadn't eaten before. It was the after-workout hunger, an insatiable appetite you feel after you have burned out your muscles. They filled their plates and started stuffing their faces, respectively looking back at me, signaling I should continue.

"I could tell he was starting to slip to a dark place. He started acting more and more out of character. He started to get in trouble with the law. One week it would be a speeding ticket and the next it would be a fight in the streets of downtown Portland. The pills continued, adding Xanax to his list of struggles. The life he was living started to spiral out of control and we did our best to help get him right."

It hurt to replay the reality of what happened. Taylor wouldn't talk about things that were bothering him. He was never openly emotional, but I could see he was hurting, struggling. He comes from a good family. His dad spent twenty years in law enforcement and served as the chief of police in Vancouver, Washington, for a number of years. His mom is an educator, a school district administrator for Portland Public Schools. That's the hardest thing about addiction. It doesn't care who you are, where you're from, or how much money you do or don't have. Addiction can affect anyone. Taylor wanted to stop, but he couldn't. Addiction is not a problem caused by the lack of willpower, but an illness that needs treatment. T-Mart became a pro at suppressing his struggles and keeping things inside while putting on a mask that made it seem like he was okay. Despite his best efforts, I could see the changes in him and it broke my heart.

Tre looked up from his pizza, young, innocent, and with a stone face.

"You still hang with him, Coach? How's he doing now?"

I paused for a moment. To this point, I hadn't spoken much about Taylor to anyone. In some ways, this was a cathartic conversation of sorts, one I hadn't expected to have with a bunch of high-schoolers, but one that I personally needed. I swallowed, choked back some of the tremendous emotions that boiled inside, and told them the truth.

"Nah . . . he passed away."

The boys weren't sure how to respond. You could tell they wondered if they had done something wrong by asking. Even though we had spent the past four weeks together, day in and day out, we hardly knew anything about each other.

"It's okay, Tre," I said. "It was last January, back in 2017. I was coaching in San Fran, and I got a call from one of our friends one evening. The first thing he said was, 'It's Taylor.' And I said, 'What happened?' He took a long pause, then said, 'He's gone.'

"That was tough. He told me Taylor had accidently overdosed. It was like a bad dream. As soon as I got off that call I was a wreck. That night I replayed our whole ten-year friendship. I thought back to how hard the last couple years had been for him. I questioned myself, could I have done more? I knew he was down bad but I was in San Francisco, I wasn't there for him."

"Damn, Coach," RJ said. "That's rough."

"You always wonder if you did enough for your friend," I said. "But I never thought it could happen to him. Things like that only become real when it happens close to you."

Life is filled with difficult lessons, but when you're young, you feel invincible. After graduating college and finishing successful football careers, Taylor and I thought we were on top of the world. But sadly, many former athletes just like Taylor end up with addiction problems. Ultimately, his problems stemmed from his surgeries, and his demons came from prescription pills. It was almost like a trap.

"I came home after Taylor passed away. It was right after the football season with the 49ers. I was coming home and didn't plan to be here for too long but ended up reflecting on my life a lot during that time. We mourned as friends and family, and as I reflected I always came back to the feeling that I just needed to be back in Portland. I was broken, and was looking for the meaning of his loss. I wasn't concerned about my career and the status of being a coach in the NFL anymore. At that time, nothing made sense to me, but home felt right.

"That fall, my brother, Trey, started his senior year of high school at Taylor's and my alma mater. Coaching and sharing the game of football with my younger brother was something that I always enjoyed and cherished. At that point I had been gone for the last seven years. I thought about all the time I'd missed and the experiences I'd never get back. I looked at the people that mattered the most to me, and they were all here in Portland. Time is something you never get back, so I made my decision.

"So that was really ultimately what brought me back. I didn't want to miss any more of the moments. The special times with my brother, friends, and family. So last year that's where I was, coaching my brother at Jesuit. I volunteered, they didn't pay me or anything. It felt right. It felt like where I was supposed to be."

The kids had stopped eating, and it was clear they were hanging on my every word. This wasn't the first time they had encountered addiction, loss, and pain. Some, if not most, had parents in jail and family members struggling with drugs and alcohol. Sadly, this was an all too familiar story. But something special happened with us at that table filled with pizza crust and chicken bones. The more I opened up to my guys, the more they respected me. We didn't just share a meal, we shared a connection.

"Coming back here, to Portland, was more for me than for anyone else. I needed it at the time. I still need it. I had a good time coaching last year, but after my brother graduated, it made sense to figure out what's next. And that's when I found you guys." I smiled and gave them a head nod. "I was a coach without a team, and you guys were a team without a coach."

I could tell, maybe for the first time over the course of our short time together, that these kids were starting to trust me. They realized I was one of them. The same experiences. The same pain. The same challenges. We were one and the same. It wasn't coach and players. We were a bunch of guys who loved football, having pizza and wings, having an honest talk about life.

I looked around at the kids as the conversation shifted to a lighter subject. I felt my best friend Taylor looking down on us. I couldn't help but think he was with me. And, in a lot of ways, Taylor was the reason why I was there at Parkrose High School, still healing and still searching for a new purpose.

3

A FATHER'S FINAL LESSON

RESPECT THE GAME

Things changed after the pizza dinner. There was a sense of urgency, dedication, and even a feeling we were becoming a family. For the first time, in likely a long time, the kids started to come together and put in the work to win. We weren't magically fixed overnight, but we were headed in the right direction.

Still months away from our first snap in a live game, our core group started to understand that the hard work they were doing now would ultimately translate to the success on the field later. As the weeks stacked up, a sense of belief was slowly building. By April, our small group of five had grown to a consistent group of ten. It was still a long way off from fifty, but they were my ten kids, and I took pride in each and every one of them.

B-Jax and I offered them a constant they'd rarely had in their lives. The strategy was working. When they chose to show up, they knew we were waiting there with open arms. No ifs, ands, or buts. We coached them hard. If they chose not to come, we never guilt-tripped them. We told them the workouts weren't mandatory and we stuck by that. The kids respected our philosophy. Together, we were stacking positive day on top of positive day.

Our relationship with our team grew as the days went by. B-Jax and I took a big brother approach, always trying to put ourselves in their shoes. From my experience, the worst coaches are the ones that belittle you and make you out to be smaller than them. That's not what this group needed, and that's not what B-Jax and I were about. Our group needed people on their side.

The more time they spent around us, the more they came to respect us not only as coaches, but as friends. B-Jax, in particular, was as cool as they come, especially to a high-schooler. Every day, fifteen minutes before workouts, he roared up to the school parking lot on his bright-red motorcycle. You could practically hear him from a few blocks away. I'm not much of a bike guy, but watching him roll right up to the gym doors on two wheels was pretty sweet. Our players thought so too. But B-Jax was much more than just a former football star turned motorcycle enthusiast. He had a special talent for inspiring and teaching young men. If you can inspire and teach, you'll probably make a helluva coach. B-Jax was a prime example of that.

At the University of Oregon, B-Jax and I were more rivals than we were friends. He was a defensive back and I was a wide receiver. For four years, every single day, we competed and battled with each other. Competition often brings out the best in you, especially on the football field, so our rivalry made us both better at our craft. Sometimes, though, it got personal.

I was a young player in my very first Fall Camp with the Ducks: four weeks in the August heat with two practices a day. At eighteen, it was the hardest, most grueling experience I had ever experienced. At that time, B-Jax, just a sophomore, was starting to make a name for himself. He played safety but hit like a linebacker. As a kid fresh out of high school, I was intimidated when I saw him lined up across from me. Coach Chip Kelly and the staff recruited him out of a national football powerhouse in Alabama: Hoover High School. B-Jax could have gone anywhere in the country to play, but chose to come out west to play for the Ducks.

During the first couple weeks of camp, I progressed slowly. The first few practices were spent mostly on my ass or getting cussed out by a coach for messing up a play. The jump from high school ball to college ball isn't supposed to be easy, and I was hanging on each day, just trying to survive and get acclimated to the way the Oregon Ducks did things.

My receivers coach, Scott Frost, had a goal that year: to make the Oregon wide receiver group the hardest-hitting receivers in the country. When we ran the football, we were expected to go put someone on their ass. I was only 165 pounds soaking wet, so personally, it was easier said than done. The only way I could put a defensive player on their bum is if I caught them when they weren't looking. Well, sure enough, my opportunity finally came, and the player that wasn't looking happened to be B-Jax. Remember how I said our rivalry got personal at times? I might have thrown the first shot.

On this particular run play, the blocking rule was simple: if the play is being run on your side, then you have an MDM, "Most Dangerous Man," block. The receiver is responsible for blocking the defensive player most likely to tackle the player with the football.

The offense called the play and my assignment was locked in.

A run play, to my side, MDM. I got into my stance, scanned the field, and locked eyes onto my target as he slowly crept forward toward the line of scrimmage. B-Jax was an instinctual player known for quickly diagnosing plays, then running downhill to make big highlight-reel tackles.

We snapped the ball and I took off like I was shot out of a rocket. B-Jax wasn't looking at me as I sprinted toward him. I lowered my shoulder into his, full speed, the sound of our pads making a *crack!* you could hear from across the practice field. B-Jax went flying, and my teammates, almost simultaneously, let out a big *"OOOOH!"* in unison.

As B-Jax was picking himself up off the ground and my offensive teammates were cheering me on, B-Jax looked at me dead in my eyes and said, "Aight bro, you want to play like that? I'm on you now."

That was the name of the game. By competing your tail off, you started to make a name for yourself. In the process, you make yourself and your teammates better. After practice, there are no hard feelings. You leave it all on the field. I caught B-Jax when he wasn't looking. For young players trying to earn a spot, that was fair game.

It didn't take long for B-Jax to get his revenge. Twenty-four hours. The very next practice he had an opportunity to take his shot, and he didn't hold back.

We called a pass play where the route design was for me to run deep across the middle. I ran my route, fifteen yards flat across the field. The quarterback threw me the ball. The pass was a little high, so I stretched my arms up over my head, exposing the middle of my body. As karma would have it, B-Jax was in the middle of the field waiting for me. As I stretched for the ball, B-Jax launched his shoulder into my overexposed rib cage. The practice field was filled with the same sound from the day before: *crack!*

But this time I was the one that got put on his ass. To the best of my ability, I acted like I wasn't fazed. I finished practice bruised and battered from the one hit I took all day. And later that evening found out B-Jax had cracked one of my ribs. The hit was legal and it was fair game. He literally lived up to the "bone-shattering" reputation he was building.

We would go back and forth over the next few years of college ball, trading shot for shot in practice, and playing side by side as brothers on game days. Over time, our personal rivalry developed into mutual respect. I came to expect the best from him, and vice versa. Years later, when I asked for his help, he didn't flinch. I would like to think our countless battles on the football field made his decision easy. Just like at practice, he knew he would get the best from me, and offer me the same.

In three months, we had our first small win: doubling our Parkrose team from five to ten. A small win, but a win nonetheless. Considering what had happened at Parkrose in the years prior, it was rare to find kids at that school that loved football, so we focused on our core group. Tre, RJ, and Taydrian would stand out from the rest. Those three became the players we could count on. They helped rally the troops and worked alongside me to convince their teammates to give B-Jax and me a chance. We were building, slowly but surely.

I walked into our afternoon workout one day and surveyed the room to see the kids warming up, stretching, and putting on their workout gear. They were clowning around, cracking jokes, and blaring hip-hop, as they often did before our weight room sessions. They were having fun, jumping up and down, and chest-bumping one another as the chorus blared from our sorry, shrunken weight room boom box.

We were light that day, with only a few players in attendance. Since we'd been finding regular momentum recently, that was strange. On our worst days, we had no less than ten players. B-Jax and I thought the days of taking attendance on one hand were gone. Once the clock struck 3:45, signaling the beginning of our session, I quieted down the room.

After looking around and taking attendance, I turned to Tay-drian, who was one of about six players who'd shown up.

"Where is everyone?" I asked. "Where's Tre and RJ?"

Tay looked around and shrugged his shoulders, unsure how to respond. I asked the others.

"Guys . . . where are they?"

No one responded.

That spring, RJ had been showing up to just about every session. He was one of the few kids that was really absorbing our coaching and buying into the new program. It was somewhat surprising, as I was cautioned that he was a kid whose attitude would sometimes surface. But we seemed to get along, and I was proud of his dedication thus far. His attitude needed to change, but the kid truly had loads of potential. Despite struggling with authority and structure, used to doing his own thing, he treated his classmates well. Tre was much the same way. He was the class clown who could sweet-talk his teachers out of anything even though he struggled with school, failing to see the importance of it like many of us do when we're young. But for Tre, football was different. Football was his sanctuary, the place where he could be himself. Up to that point, he hadn't missed a single day.

It was as if the guys got together and collectively decided they were going to skip the workout. As coaches, we worked so hard to institute some level of consistency; every day we seemed to be making progress. So when the kids didn't show, especially after we were beginning to trend in the right direction, something had to change. Looking at our depleted numbers, I knew I had to track Tre and RJ down.

"You guys go ahead and continue stretching," I told the players in the weight room. "We're going to go find the other guys." Then I told B-Jax, "Let's go find these kids. They didn't go home. These kids don't just go home after school, they're somewhere."

With that, we stormed out of the weight room on a mission to locate our players and get their butts in the weight room. The first stop was the basketball court. We opened the gym doors and saw three of our kids in the middle of a pickup basketball game. I thought to myself, *You got to be kidding me.*

B-Jax walked right into the middle of their game and yelled out at them, "Hey! We got workouts, man, let's go!"

The three basketball culprits, with shock in their eyes, immediately jumped out of the game and grabbed their backpacks from the sideline. They walked past me out through the gym doors, avoiding eye contact.

"Sorry, Coach Lowe," they blurted out.

We were gaining traction now—ten minutes after our scheduled start time—but we were still missing some key players. We made our way from the gym to the hallways. Sitting on the back staircase with his buddies, we found none other than Tre Singleton.

"So we're not coming to workouts today or what, Tre? I never thought you'd skip football," I said sarcastically. He felt bad, but only because he got caught. He knew he was wrong, so he kept it short.

"My bad. On my way, Coach."

As he walked down the hallway in the direction of the weight room, B-Jax hollered out one more message: "You're better than that, Tre!"

Before that day, we had been lenient about attendance and didn't demand too much of the team. If I pushed too hard early on, there was a chance the players would show up once and never again. Mr. Shelton did a good job of explaining to me the general attitude of our students, so I planned accordingly. I needed these guys to want to play rather than feel like it was something they were being forced to do, so I made adjustments, instituting open workouts and allowing players to show up whenever they wanted. It seemed to be working, but had now become a slippery slope. Time had come for a change. We had to show the players they had to get serious about what we were trying to help them build at Parkrose.

We walked around other parts of campus, finding more players. We pulled kids off the basketball courts, and from in front of the school. Just like we expected, our guys were nearby the weight room, still on the school premises. After the hustle around the school, we ultimately found about fifteen players to rejoin our workout group. We got no pushback from any of them.

That is, until I finally found my boy RJ.

B-Jax and I walked through the cafeteria one last time and saw RJ sitting at a table with a group of his friends.

I made a beeline for him.

"Yo RJ, we got lifting, man. What are you doing? Let's go, we're late."

He looked at me, partially shocked and partially embarrassed I'd called him out in front of his friends.

"I'm good, Coach," he said. "I will catch y'all tomorrow."

RJ was used to adults backing down, taking his shit, and leaving him alone. But not today. I didn't have time.

"You said you want to be great, right?" I asked, while the group of kids sat there and listened intently.

He stood up, raised his voice and challenged me.

"I said I'm good, Lowe."

I didn't back off. "What, you don't want to work?"

"Yeah, I want to work!" RJ snapped back, with a prideful look, as if I were the crazy one for even asking the question.

"Do you want to be good?" I asked. "Do you want to get better?"

"Yeah, I want to get better."

He didn't mean it. It was clear from the way he said it.

"Man, you don't want to get better," I said, shaking my head.

Everyone got quiet, looking on at the confrontation. Most of the kids didn't know me all that well, so they must have been thinking, *Who's this new coach?* None of these students played football; they weren't sure what to make of me. But there was RJ, right in front of all his buddies and girlfriends, trying to be the cool kid of the bunch.

"You don't want to work," I said. I was pushing back, not taking his nonsense defense mechanisms and excuses. "You're afraid. You're afraid to put in the work. You're afraid of the work. Stop lying to yourself."

And in that moment, the truth hurt. I saw it in his face. No one had ever kept it real with him like that, especially not a football coach. Mind you, their old football coaches were nearly nonexistent. They showed up to practice late and didn't care about the kids or their growth and success. Players would walk all over them, often showing up and leaving whenever they felt like it.

I saw RJ for who he was: a confident kid who needed some tough love. He needed help to develop his confidence and hone it. More so than that type of love, he also needed the truth. RJ reminded me of the thousands of young athletes across the country that say they want something but don't put their actions toward achieving it. RJ and my other players had to learn a simple lesson. Your goals and your actions must align.

He stood there with his fist clenched like he wanted to throw hands. RJ fumed. The kids at the lunch table looked on in shock. The anger and rage were boiling within him.

WHAP! He slammed his hand on the lunch table, pressed forward, and yelled out, "You don't know nothing!!!"

Sensing I had made my point, I looked at him, this time speaking in a straightforward yet calm voice. "When you decide that you want to get better, you know where to find us." And then I walked away, leaving B-Jax standing there between us.

In that moment, I had to stand up to RJ. I had to put my foot down. B-Jax and I were a great team, playing good cop / bad cop. After I walked away, B-Jax stepped forward, put his arm around RJ, and took him to the side. RJ was emotional but B-Jax reeled him in. He took the time to talk him down and explain to him where I was coming from. He spoke to RJ in simple terms: We were building a team, and he would either be a part of it and do the right thing or there wouldn't be a place for him on the squad. The choice would be his and his alone. B-Jax had a way with getting through to these young men when they needed it most.

I quickly made it back to the weight room. I'd been away for twenty minutes tracking down my team, and now I could finally start the workouts with the guys that were ready to go. As we were running through a superset between incline press and push-ups, B-Jax and RJ walked into the room together. RJ walked in and hopped into the workout. Whatever B-Jax said got through to him. At that point, I knew I didn't need to say another word. He didn't look at me. He didn't make eye contact with me. Hell, he probably hated me in that moment. None of that mattered. He showed up and he started to work out with his teammates, and that's all I could ask. We had an understanding.

RJ didn't talk to me for a week, but he didn't miss a single workout either. He showed up and was never late. He didn't want to talk to me, and I didn't press on him or push him about it. I didn't need that. I just needed him to understand that if you wanted to accomplish something, then you had to take the right steps in order to do so. You can't lie to yourself by saying you are doing the work and expect to succeed.

I made it a point to hold each and every single player on our team accountable. It didn't matter who you were, how talented you were on the field, or how important you might be to the success of the team. No one received preferential treatment, and everyone answered to the same expectations. RJ was no different. Now, there might have been times when I was harder on RJ than some of the other kids, but in many ways, it was justified. I'd spoken to folks around Parkrose, and the kid was on a downward spiral and wasn't on track to graduate. If he ever had a chance to turn things around, he'd have to control his emotions and be accountable for his actions.

Little did he know it at the time, but me and RJ had a lot in common. We weren't that different. We both came from biracial families, with white moms and Black dads. Neither of us had our dads around growing up. RJ had two older sisters, and I had one. He was the youngest, the baby of the family. That might explain some of his behavior: he was used to always getting his way. RJ lived in a poor part of town, and had to struggle with some of the same environmental challenges I'd experienced growing up as well.

He had an infectious personality, and was a genuinely good kid. We were similar in that regard. In many ways, it all came down to accountability. Even having similar backgrounds, I often wondered, why had I stayed in the straight and narrow, and he strayed? Why did I respect authority while he ran from it? If I could control my emotions and show up, why couldn't RJ get out of his own way?

Even though my father wasn't in my life for the long run, he was present for the first eight years. I once heard that the first seven years of your life are the most formative, that you're a sponge at the time. You soak everything around you up and those experiences begin to shape who you are. I had my dad during that time, which helped to build structure. He was always teaching me lessons and feeding me with ideas. We'd watch football together, and he'd excitedly point to the television and say, "Hey, that's going to be you one day. You're going to be catching the ball on the field. You're going to get a scholarship!" I didn't even know what a scholarship was, but he told me from a young age that I was going to get one. "You're going to get a scholarship, a full ride. That's going to be you playing on TV."

And I believed him. I didn't know how hard that would actually be, or if I could actually do that, but I believed him. My father used football to teach me many life lessons as a kid. By the time my family structure blew up, I was already strong and account-able. I'll forever be grateful to my dad for that.

RJ didn't have that same accountability from a young age. He was seventeen years old and lacked a solid foundation. It wasn't his fault, but it was absolutely the difference between my childhood and his. On top of that, I had a little brother. When my dad left home, whether I was ready for it or not, I became the miniature man of the house. My little brother, eight years younger than me, was born just as my father was leaving. When he came into this world, I felt accountable for him. There were things happening with my parents, and tension at home that I couldn't explain. But one thing I did know is that my little bro would be just like me, in all the good ways and all the bad ways. So I wanted to give him a good person to be like. From even a young age, I knew he was watching and learning, ready to repeat my behavior. It offered a strange and very complicated sense of accountability. Knowing your actions impact and affect someone else often shapes the way you act.

When it came to RJ, I always wondered if having a younger brother or sister would have forced him to look at himself a lit-tle bit more. Maybe it would have helped him decide to do the right thing more often. We both had great moms, constants in our homes. When you have a single mom, working multiple jobs, you innately want to do everything you can to make her home life eas-ier. But that extra layer of accountability from my little brother, as well as the foundation my dad built before he left us, really put me in a place to succeed.

The confrontation with RJ put me in a headspace to reflect on my own life. Even after I'd left the weight room, I found my-self thinking about the difficulties and sacrifices that had defined my own childhood. Over the course of the first six years of my life, we lived in an apartment complex, just a few minutes away from Parkrose High School. My sister, who is two years older than me, went to kindergarten in the Parkrose district. I always thought that was kind of ironic, how I ended up back where I started. From there we moved into a house in Gresham, a middle- to lower-income town about twenty minutes east of Portland. When my little bro was born, we became a family of five.

My dad and his struggles, mostly alcohol-related, made him unstable and angry. On his best days he was my hero, but on his worst I barely recognized him. My parents fought loudly every night. Nothing violent, as far as I know, but there were lots of sleepless nights filled with screaming past midnight. It wasn't easy to grow up in a home with an alcoholic father. A disease like alcoholism affects your family first and foremost. My mom couldn't count on him anymore and their marriage started to fall apart. He had his good moments, but he also had some pretty terrible ones. He would be at home with us, then get into some trouble and disappear for a few days, or weeks, or months. Then he'd be back home, like nothing ever happened, and the cycle would repeat itself.

Since we lived so close to school and my mom was always working, it wasn't uncommon for me to walk to and from school. We were in a rather safe neighborhood after moving to Gresham, so all the neighborhood kids walked home on their own. I was walking home from elementary school one day—I must've been in the third grade—when one of the neighborhood kids walked up to me and said, "What happened to your dad?" Obviously, I had no clue what he was talking about. I froze, confused, but innately knew I needed to walk faster. So I picked up the pace, despite my oversized backpack dragging me down.

I turned the corner to the cul-de-sac and saw a police car out in front of our house. I stopped in my tracks when I saw it, unsure how to react. This wasn't the first time I witnessed the police at my house, so I wasn't going to stick around to find out what happened. I instantly turned around and walked back to my school. When I got there, I went to the swing set and sat, head down with tears in my eyes. I wasted as much time as I could, hoping whatever was happening at my house would be over with by the time I decided to go back. I didn't know what to do. I was too young to understand, but I knew one thing: that car was there for my hero.

I loved my dad. He gave me so much, but he was just too sick to remain a constant in my life at that time. However, I was never mad at him for that. In middle school, I started to understand that just because people have problems or are suffering doesn't mean they're bad people. My dad was the first example of that for me. He was in a dark place. He was suffering. The alcohol would get the best of him on most days, causing him to be inconsistent in our lives. That's at least, in part, why I sympathized with my best friend Taylor. I never did blame him for the decisions that led him to accidentally take his own life. After a while, he couldn't control it, just like my dad couldn't control his alcoholism.

So many highs and so many lows. And then one day, he was gone. I think that happens to a lot of kids. One day I realized, *Oh, I haven't seen Dad recently. He hasn't been home in a while.* My mom never sat us down to talk about it. Sometimes what's understood doesn't have to be said. We were young, so there wasn't a big dramatic moment where it all came to a head. It just kind of happened.

The world simply continued on for us. I navigated school and grew more and more comfortable in my own skin. After my dad left, my parents separated, and we had to downsize our home. We stayed in Gresham so not a lot changed in our daily lives—same schools, same extracurriculars. That's when I started to take football seriously, mostly because I wanted to be like the guys me and my dad watched on television. And, of course, to get that full-ride scholarship (even though I still didn't know what that was). We moved again when I was in the fifth grade: me, my older sister, younger brother, and my mom. The four of us didn't have much, but we had each other and that was more than enough.

My sister, Alisa, and I picked up the slack to make sure our little brother was always accounted for. Having a single parent was a blessing in a way. It forced me and my sister to think about each other more than we thought about ourselves. When adversity struck, it affected all of us. We went through it together and grew closer from it. We became battle-tested.

With my dad out of the picture, there were no more days where we would throw the ball in the front yard for hours. No more football games on Sundays, no more field-trip chaperone. I often lay in my bed at night wishing and praying he was somewhere safe. That he was okay. For years, I channeled the sadness into football. At times it felt like it was all I had, and to be honest, it was all I needed. I became addicted. Always in the back of my mind was my dad. I was going to make him proud, wherever he was. Who knows, maybe one day I would inspire him enough to get clean.

They say your life is often defined by a few pivotal moments. One of those moments came when I was in the seventh grade. We had family that lived in Beaverton, a suburb of Portland on the west side. Beaverton felt like a different planet, even though it was a quick forty-five-minute drive from where we lived. It was the week of the OSAA State Football Quarterfinal games and my big cousin, Michael Remy, was scheduled to play. I only got to see Michael a couple times a year, but in a lot of ways, he was doing what I always wanted to do. He was three years older, an all-state baseball player *and* an all-state receiver. He was the man at the top high school in Oregon, Jesuit High School.

Jesuit High School is a Catholic college-preparatory school in the middle of Beaverton. The academic regime was rigorous and the sports programs were the best in the state. That fateful Friday night, when my mom took me to watch my big cousin play in the state football playoffs, I thought I was walking into a regular high school game, but boy was I wrong. It was electric, like nothing I had seen before. I watched Michael catch touchdown passes in those shiny gold helmets. For all I knew, I was watching the Fighting Irish of Notre Dame go up and down that field. At twelve years old, I finally had a clear path.

On the car ride home, I told my mom I wanted to play football at Jesuit High School, like Michael. While I had no context or understanding as to what that meant or would require, I couldn't help but see myself on the field with those gold helmets. As a seventh-grader from Gresham, I had no idea what *private, college prep,* or *Catholic* was, but I knew it looked like the right place for me. Football practice was where I would go and feel free and escape the challenges around me. I didn't have to take care of anybody except myself, and that was where I let everything out. I became a dawg. A nice guy off the field, but an asshole in between the lines. I was able to express myself and to make my dad proud, whether he was watching or not.

One day, weeks after that Friday night, my mom sat me down out of the blue. She looked at me after dinner and said, "Do you really want to go to Jesuit?" She proceeded to explain to me what kind of high school Jesuit was.

"What's a Catholic school?" I asked. "What does college preparatory mean?"

She was always really good at breaking things down for me.

My last question: "What's a private school?"

She paused for a moment, carefully selecting the words in her head. "Well, a private school is a school that's only open to a select few," she explained. "Usually, you have to apply and be chosen. And once you're selected, it costs money every year to attend."

"A lot of money?" I asked. The concept of a high school that cost money was foreign to me.

She stopped me and asked again, "Do you really want to go? Don't worry about the money. If you really want this, Keanon, then I can make it happen. But only if this is what you want."

I didn't know much, but I knew enough to realize my mom would have to move her and her three kids across town to Beaverton. Not only would she have to find a new job, but she would have to find us a place to live and a way to pay for me to go to school. But I trusted my mom and she trusted me. Maybe she saw it in my eyes, or maybe she was looking for a fresh start away from Gresham. Either way, she told me not to worry, so I didn't.

"I want to go, Mom. Let's do it."

When someone you love leaves your life, it is quite the shock. You always think they'll be there forever; you never expect it to end. My kids at Parkrose understood loss as well. Many of them didn't have parents present in the home, had lost loved ones to violence, and knew what it was like to mourn and miss. Personally, I always thought my dad would be around forever. Even in the ups and the downs, I just assumed he'd stumble back into the house, grab dinner, and sit back down on the couch to watch a game with me. When that didn't happen, I realized there'd be a void I would never fill. But even so, I will never forget the last lesson he taught me. Still young, I was very impressionable. It became a funny quote he would say, almost in a joking way:

"You better respect the game . . . or the game ain't gonna respect you."

He would say it so often that I would finish his sentence whenever he decided to drop his one-liner. It became our thing, our inside joke that became my real-life motto. He would look at me, with a shoulder shrug, a head tilt, and a side-eye: "You better respect the game . . ."

And I, with my little high-pitched voice, would snap back, "Or the game ain't gonna respect you!"

Those were just words to me as a child, but as I got older I found them to be profound. I applied them to my passion, football, and how I approached the game. I respected the game and the process before "the process" was a thing. I knew I had to impart this lesson to my players at Parkrose. They weren't used to putting in the work, following the process, and recognizing incremental improvement.

How do you show respect to the game of football? I answered that question with my actions. To me, it was quite simple. You practice and play your ass off every chance you get. You appreciate and take advantage of each opportunity because you never know if it will be your last. I was fortunate enough to figure one central truth out at a young age, a lesson that I would try to hammer into RJ and the rest of my kids at Parkrose: The more you put into something, the more you get out of it. The harder you work, the more your hard work will be rewarded. You don't get good at something by accident. The more respect you show to your craft, the more your craft will respect you.

My dad's silly motto became a way of life for me. As I grew older, the saying evolved from, "Respect the game of football" to "Respect the *game of life*." I wanted people to treat me with respect so I showed respect to others. I wanted people to help me if I was in need, so I always supported others. As I matured, I started to appreciate the gift of life. I wanted good things to happen to me. And for good things to happen to me, I understood I had to be a good person to other people. At Parkrose those people were my players: RJ, Tre, and all the rest.

4

RUNNING THE "9"

FATE REWARDS SHOWING UP

As the spring season gave way to a hot Portland summer, we started to face the reality of our squad. Most of our players hadn't played a great deal of football. Some were new to the game, others were never taught the fundamentals. We were starting from square one, even with the most talented players in the program.

On the last day of school before summer break, we gathered the team in the weight room for a football sign-up meeting. Earlier that week, I'd spent my time making and posting an excessive number of flyers across the school hallways and walls. This meeting was mandatory if you wanted to officially play ball for the Broncos, since we needed to collect contact info and pass out the summer workout schedule. But as always, B-Jax and I wondered what the turnout would be. The last time I had the bright idea to make and post flyers around the school, it turned out to be a huge dud. If at first you don't succeed, I told myself, try again.

"How many you thinkin' today, Coach?" B-Jax asked as we took our place outside the weight room doors. The final bell of the school year rang.

I could sense the sarcasm in his voice, but we remained hopeful our guys would show up for us. Sure enough, one after the other, our new football team filed into the weight room, each one giving us a handshake as they walked in the doorway. There were even kids I had never seen before. Each player wrote their name and phone number on the sign-up sheet. Then, we all huddled in the middle of the musty room.

Once the traffic through the sign-up sheet slowed down, and before I addressed the team, I turned to B-Jax to find out how many names we had on the piece of notebook paper. With a shocked face, he looked to me from across the room.

"Forty-five," B-Jax mouthed.

Pleasantly surprised with the turnout, I took the center of the room and quieted the guys down. "Alright boys, listen up, listen up, lock in."

As the chatter came to a stop, Tre shouted out, "Hats and hoods!"

The team followed Tre's direction and removed their hats and hoods from their heads in unison. I looked at Tre and gave him a subtle head nod and continued.

"Look guys . . . we are heading into the most important part of the year, the summer." I can't lie, it felt really good to address a group this big again. Over the last couple of months, it seemed like B-Jax and I were doing more personal training than actually coaching a team. "I look around this room and see a bunch of young men that want to play. That want to be a part of what we're building. You made the choice to show up today and that's what this thing's all about. You have a choice, every single day, of what kind of person and what kind of teammate you want to be."

As I chatted, B-Jax pulled a large stack of paper from his gym bag. He disbursed a few smaller sets to the outreached arms of the kids, and they passed it around and began to study it.

"In front of you is your summer workout calendar. To this day we haven't made our workouts mandatory. You could show up when you wanted to. Take a day off and no one was on your ass. But now, now, you have to commit."

Many of them were fixated on the paper in front of them. Some looked like they were in pain, but others were excited to have a path for getting out on the field.

"If you want to be on this team, you will commit to the schedule on the paper in front of you. Is that all clear?"

In unison, the group of forty-five responded, "Yes, Coach."

"If you stick through this thing, it's going to be worth it. If you just listen to me, if you do everything I'm asking you to do, we're going to win, I promise you that. The things you boys go through, the shit you've been through, that's what makes you different. There isn't a team in the state that's as tough as the group I'm looking at right now, and I'm not even talking football right now."

The weight room started to fill with that same optimistic energy and buzz reminiscent of the first time I met these boys in the auditorium. They were locked in and absorbing every word. After months of chasing and herding these kids around, they finally showed up for me. Altogether, forty-five strong.

"Each and every one of you has something special to offer. All of us have things we've been through, we all have a personal story. But right now, we have the opportunity to write our own story, as one."

Together they all nodded their heads up and down in agreement.

"I'm going to simplify this thing for you guys. In order to play on this team, for Coach Jackson and I, you have to follow three rules: *show up, put in the work,* and *don't make excuses.* In life, half the battle is showing up and sometimes that's the hardest thing to do."

That was real. For my guys taking multiple city buses in the summer mornings, it would be difficult. It'd probably be the hardest part of their summer days. But when you play a team sport, you have a responsibility to show up for the other members of your team. There is no secret to success. If you're willing to show up and put in the work, you can get anything in life that you desire. I would be determined to ingrain this life lesson into the core of each and every young person I had the privilege of coaching.

"And maybe the most important rule: don't make excuses . . . Look, I get it, I know we don't have the nicest weight room and equipment. Other schools have turf fields and we have to play on grass. We don't have this, and we don't have that . . . but fellas, that's all bullshit. We can't control those things. But what we can control is our attitude and our effort. The other teams we'll line up against have to tie their cleats and buckle up that chinstrap just like us!"

The words were directed at the young men standing in front of me, but in reality, that message was for myself. I had a lot to prove. I wanted to prove to these kids, my family, and my city that I could build these troubled young men into a team: not just a team, but a winning team. And the only way to do it was by living out every single word I preached. My personal strategy was simple: outwork every other coach in the state, throw so much energy into these kids that they would feed off it, and believe in them so strongly that they would have no choice but to naturally start believing in each other, and most importantly, believe in themselves.

"Parkrose has allowed you all to be comfortable in a culture of quitting. Well, those times are over. We are a team now. And I believe in what this group can do. Make no mistake, this group standing in front of me is going to change the culture of our school."

The kids started clapping, hollering, and yelling out loud. They were juiced. We had spent just a few months together, but you could tell that we were on the road to building something special. In a week's time, we would be back in that weight room to officially start the journey.

The weight room was beat down and falling apart, but at least it didn't lack personality. The walls were covered with chipped white paint. The pull-up bars had screws falling out of the wall. The old, mismatched dumbbell sets had been donated by a local gym. It was ugly but it was all we had, so we took advantage of it. The unique room sat on top of the gym, overlooking the basketball court. Often you would look out and see kids hanging out on the bleachers or playing basketball after school. On the same level, just outside the weight room doors, a small cement track surrounded the upper outer edges of the gym. Spray-painted in green letters on the white brick walls above that track: "9½ laps = 1 mile." *The Nine,* as my players would come to know, represented the nine full laps a player would run if he chose to show up late to practice.

On our first full day of summer workouts, B-Jax and I arrived at 8:30 A.M. to get set up. Our summer workout schedule was straightforward. We would hold workouts four days a week, always starting with a weight room session before transitioning to the field for speed and agility work. As I stood in the middle of the weight room, I watched three-quarters of the team trickle in with their duffle bags and football cleats over their shoulders. B-Jax chased after them, reminding the kids that they'd either be on time or run nine laps around the cement track.

I positioned myself in the weight room at 9 A.M., surrounded by the guys that showed up on time. The rest of our players would run upon arrival, facing the harsh reality that they'd start their practice by paying the brass tacks of running the Nine. It didn't matter if you were one minute late or one hour late. Show up past 9 A.M. and you were running. It didn't take B-Jax but a split second to raise his hand in the air and move it in a circular motion, signaling that it was time to drop your gear and start running. Once they were done, they could jump right back into the workout. Pay the price, serve the punishment, and fall in. If you don't want to run, then show up on time. It was really that simple.

We'd start every workout day with a twenty-minute warm-up. That was the easiest part of our mornings: getting the muscles ready for the two-hour workday ahead. As I surveyed the kids, I realized that RJ, now fifteen minutes into our first day of summer, still hadn't showed. It felt as if we had turned a corner together, but this type of behavior seemed to be impossible to shake. One step forward, two steps back.

Up until this point, RJ had really turned things around. We had our differences but over the course of the last few months we were able to find common ground. He finished the spring strong, and we expected that he would start the summer workout season in similar form. Clearly, though, that wouldn't be the case. He was back to his old ways.

As I focused on getting the kids warmed up for practice, I looked to the far side of the weight room. I could see RJ, who looked every bit of a football player, nonchalantly walking in the doors with his headphones over his ears and chin held high. He had no giddyup in his step. He leisurely sat on a chair, took off his slides, and changed into his workout shoes. All while taking his sweet time. He clearly couldn't care less that he was late on the first day.

B-Jax, seeing RJ move in slow motion, confronted him. I watched on, one eye on their exchange, the other on my players warming up. Even from a distance, it was clear things were starting to get pretty heated between the two of them. What started as a relatively calm exchange turned into a full onslaught of shouting. B-Jax remained himself, calm and collected, while RJ refused to run the Nine. It was clear he was looking for a fight.

I couldn't believe what I saw next.

RJ, still half-dressed, reached back and threw a punch at B-Jax. Now remember, B-Jax was a hell of a college safety, and by most measurements a pretty intimidating guy, so it took a lot of disregard for RJ to take a shot at him. Naturally, and without much effort, B-Jax easily dodged the haymaker. The kid was lucky B-Jax had restraint and didn't kick his ass into the dirt right then and there. Still in shock, B-Jax kept his composure and peacefully calmed RJ down to prevent any further fighting. After B-Jax physically calmed him down, RJ stormed out of practice. As quick as he came, he left.

We didn't miss a beat. I looked back at the kids warming up and those still running the Nine.

"Let's go! Nothing to see over there. He is gone. Focus on what's in front of you!"

B-Jax looked at me, shrugged his shoulders, and shook his head. It only took twenty minutes for something to go wrong. But hey, we were used to rolling with the punches by now. We brushed it off and kept pushing.

These types of lash-outs were common at Parkrose. In many ways, it wasn't the players' fault at all. Every kid in my program was dealing with other challenges in their lives outside of school and football. Frankly, many of them lacked the tools a young person needs in order to cope with those things. As their new coach the best thing I could do is show up for them consistently, be honest, and hold them accountable if they started to slip. Although life may be difficult at times, that is never an excuse for poor behavior. It's also not an excuse to give up on yourself. I knew I couldn't save every kid at Parkrose, but I was confident I could make a difference in the lives of my players. They hadn't won a game in three years and were wholly abandoned by most male figures in their lives. Because of that, I always felt they deserved a second, third, and even a fourth chance.

We had to be patient. Just like trust, structure also takes time to build and it starts with showing up to your obligations on time, hence the Nine. Up to that point they had done things however they wanted. They certainly hadn't had any sense of guidance on the football field. It would be unrealistic for me to expect they'd all just fall in line and become perfect little angels. We wouldn't tolerate any of this childish behavior, but we would always give the players as many chances as they needed as long as they didn't quit. Sure, you could hold these boys accountable for their actions, but it is hard to blame a young man who has seen no better way, through no fault of his own.

Understanding that early on helped me mentally prepare to go into Parkrose with thick skin. I would make it a point, within myself, to never give up on these guys. Every passing day tested my willpower, but I was determined to stay true to my sentiment.

RJ showed up the next day, on time, and didn't say a word. He was geared up and put in one of the best sessions of the summer. I loved the aggression he had. In the game of football, the aggressor often wins. My challenge was helping him deal with that aggression outside of the lines. He snapped at times, but I could deal with that. Did it hurt the team? Of course it did. But in certain rare situations, it makes sense to put an individual before the team by giving them multiple chances, as strange as that sounds. He needed B-Jax and me, and we understood that. The easy decision would be to kick him off the team right then and there, but taking the easy way out was never my style, especially when someone needed me. And besides, I saw something in RJ that he hadn't yet seen in himself. I still believed in him and the powerful lessons that can be learned from football.

We marched on. Each day presented a new set of challenges and unexpected circumstances. In the weight room, though, B-Jax was a magician. We only had one squat rack, two bars, and two benches, but ultimately it didn't matter. If you asked B-Jax to create an all-encompassing full-body workout using only sticks and rocks, I'd be willing to bet he could do it. No equipment? No problem. Every day he came with something fresh and new to keep the boys interested. The workouts were challenging, made up of body-weight exercises and plyometrics. I knew they were challenging because B-Jax and I were right there in the trenches with these boys, grinding side by side like the old days.

How do you teach young people the proper way to work out? Simple answer: you get off your high horse and you show them. They hadn't yet witnessed how pushing through pain could be rewarding, and ultimately fun. They didn't understand how to get excited when someone on the team hit their personal best. So, we showed them. Dripping sweat, jumping up and down, and yelling at the top of our lungs, we did the workouts alongside our young soldiers. The adults and administrators that walked past those weight room windows probably thought we were out of our minds, but B-Jax and I were in our element. We were there to help these boys build something they could be proud of. We were there to set an example for them, and our growing relationship with our boys kept them coming back.

Thankfully, I was soon able to add another coach. Brian Alves had been a part of that school for the last seven years. "Alves" was the glue that kept Parkrose High School together, an unsung, underappreciated hero that worked tirelessly behind the scenes to make things go smoothly. He worked as a security guard and the head coach of the depleted wrestling program. If a problem popped up at the school, Alves was sent to solve it. He knew this school and community better than anyone else, and soon became a trustworthy friend.

The school fights, the thefts, the class-skippers—Alves was in charge of resolving all of that. The teachers and administrators trusted him, but more importantly every kid at Parkrose confided in him. From the school's biggest troublemakers to the straight-A students, Alves was loved. He was an ally for every person that walked through those doors, including me. When I learned he was a great dude with a soft spot for the kids in the community, it was a no-brainer to get him on board. Later on, he would nonchalantly reveal he played DII football at Western Oregon University in his heyday. To say I was lucky to have Alves be a part of my staff would be an understatement. He fit right into what B-Jax and I were about. He was there to serve these young people, even in the roughest of times, and he did so with pride.

As we ground out the early weeks of summer workouts, Vice Principal Drake Shelton often left his summer school duties to come down and check in on me.

"Coach Lowe, I see you! You're changing the culture around here!" He pulled me to the side just as we were finishing up a day's work.

Still trying to catch my breath and sweat still dripping from my forehead, I said, "Man, I'm trying, but we still got a *long* way to go." I took a sip of Gatorade and wiped my mouth. "You weren't lying though . . . nothing comes easy around this place. I'm hanging in there though."

"Ah stop, you're doing a great job, brother. What you have going on, right now, at this time of year . . . it's nothing but amazing." He put his hand on my shoulder in a big-brother type of way. "The hardest part about my job is once summer hits, there's no telling where my students are or what they're getting into," Drake said. "It keeps me up at night. Three months without seeing them, I just pray they stay on the right path. But you're keeping them close, you and B-Jax are giving them a reason to be here! I wish we could help you out a little more." He motioned to the broken-down equipment in our line of vision. "But you know how it is, things are tight around here."

By now, I knew exactly how it was. "We'll be alright," I said. "As long as we got a ball and some grass, we'll find a way."

"Yes, sir, no doubt about it. But anyways, to the point . . . I wanted to come up here and check on you, not the kids."

I was curious what he meant by that. "I'm all good, Drake. Always."

"What you doing for work? I know you can't survive on this five-thousand-dollar stipend. For the number of hours you put in, you're basically doing this for free!"

When someone gets into high school coaching, it's a safe bet that they aren't doing it for the money. The individuals that make the decision to coach high school sports do so because they love molding young people through the sport they fell in love with as children. I was no different. I believed in the power of football, and I was at a point in my life where I was essentially willing to coach for free.

"I'm solid," I responded without hesitation. "I got money saved up, got a little part-time job. I'm making it work."

I was hoping I wouldn't get asked that question. To be honest, I was making it work, but I was just barely scraping by. My part-time job was humbling. I worked at a place called the Multnomah Athletic Club, or the MAC. For people in Portland, the MAC is known for its swanky members and rich bloodlines. Essentially, it's a country club smack-dab in the middle of the city with an absurd yearly fee and an even more outlandish waiting list to join. The club was massive. On one side of the building there were first-class Olympic pools, racquetball, tennis, and basketball courts. Not to mention a beautiful workout facility for cardio and weight lifting. The other side of the club held the event spaces: ballrooms, meeting rooms, lounges, and a five-star restaurant.

Just a year ago, when I lost my boy Taylor and every motivation to continue to pursue a career in the coaching business, I made the decision to come back home, knowing I would eventually need to figure out a way to support myself. Once the dust settled, I picked myself up and figured it out. I wanted my afternoons freed up so I could coach. I looked into blue-collar minimum-wage jobs where I could earn a decent paycheck but not get sucked into the typical nine-to-five rat race. I ran from any job posting that said "salary." I refused to apply for an office job or something that would steal the hours of my day away, especially if I didn't love doing it.

My search brought me to a job posting at the MAC. Hourly pay, early mornings, and a potential for health benefits if I put enough time in. Sign me up. The hours would be 5 to 11 A.M. with some weekend and evening shifts sprinkled in. The job title: Event Operations Setup. I was in charge of working on a two-man team that was responsible for prepping and cleaning the event spaces. The events varied from small meeting room setups to giant five-hundred-chair parties spread across fifty tables. For those, we had to build entire dance floors and put up stages. And once those meetings or events concluded, it was our responsibility to stack the chairs, restore the tables, and clean the room once more.

It's a humbling experience to go from coaching on an NFL sideline to vacuuming rooms and cleaning off tables for rich folks. But it was a part of my journey and, frankly, it put money in my pockets so I could do what I loved to do.

I didn't work every day, so on my off-days I would pop in to Parkrose at lunchtime and hang out with Drake and the kids. On the days I did work, it was nothing less than a grind. I appreciated

Drake coming and checking on me. It was clear he not only cared about the kids but he cared about me as well.

"Look, Coach," he continued. "I might have an opportunity for you down the road after Christmas break."

"January?" I asked.

"Yep, it would be this January. I know it's a ways out but I wanted to put it on your radar. See if you might be interested at all . . . it's an opportunity to work at the school."

He knew I didn't have a teaching degree, so I was sure it wasn't an opportunity in the classroom.

"What position you thinking?" I asked, genuinely curious.

"You would be working alongside Brian Alves as a security guard."

As soon as the words left his mouth, I accidently thought out loud and blurted, "Security!?"

He was serious. "One of our longtime security guards is thinking about retiring after fall term. The job is nothing flashy, but hey, it's full-time, you would get an opportunity to work with other students outside of your football team, and to be honest, I think you can make an impact with our student body. The more we can have Coach Lowe around, the better for us."

He made a good point. I never saw myself working as a security guard, but then again, I never thought I'd be taking out trash and vacuuming floors for a living either. Not ready to commit to anything so far away, I thanked Drake for looking out.

"I'll think about it," I said.

As we hit the midway point of summer practices, I started to see change in these young men. B-Jax and I continued to fight the battle, but we were getting through to them more often than not.

As expected, we lost a couple players who couldn't just skate by anymore. We were building, brick by brick. This mismatched and often-judged group of kids were coming together and becoming a team. They were still running the Nine far too often, and still had their individual blowups at times, but we were growing in a positive direction. I stayed inspired.

We started the summer with forty-five kids, but whittled our group down to about thirty-five by midsummer. Every week it seemed like a kid would fall off and never show up again. It's not easy to wake up early in the summer knowing other kids are sleeping in. The weight room, the conditioning, the accountability: it's a tough sport. When it comes to my love of football, I'm as biased as they come. But I'm confident it was the primary reason I was able to battle through challenging times when life threw them at me. To play this game you have to be tough, whether you're a high-schooler or an NFL player. Playing football prepares you for the challenges of life because no matter who you are or where you're from, life is tough.

Every single day you play this game, it's a battle. Whether or not the person lined up across from you is bigger, faster, or stronger, you are forced to battle. But the biggest battle on the football field is between your ears, the one you fight within yourself. When your brain is telling you to quit or give up, how do you respond? The longer you play this game and the more internal battles you fight, the more calloused your mind becomes. Football forces you to confront your adversities. It's a sport where you literally and figuratively have to pick yourself up off the ground over and over again. That process teaches you things about yourself that you may not have otherwise learned. That's what this thing is all about.

Every day the message was clear. If you follow our three rules—show up, put in the work, and don't make excuses—then you will succeed. Not only a recipe for success in football, but a recipe for success in life.

On a midsummer Friday, we finished B-Jax's grueling workout and came together for one last message before the weekend.

"Everyone stand in a circle, side by side," I instructed.

We all moved together in unison. Once the circle was formed I looked at B-Jax, giving him a slight head nod. He had the floor.

B-Jax walked to the middle of the circle. The kids went quiet as he took his place. He then looked at the group and began in his Alabama accent, "Listen boys, I'm proud of how far we've come. But we are just barely scratching the surface." He paced around slowly in the middle of the circle, making sure to make eye contact with every young man there. "I got a question for you . . . what is the first thing you have to do when you're building a house?"

The kids looked around at each other, unsure of who would be the first brave soul to answer the question. Tony, an undersized freshman of Asian descent, wearing his trademark gold chain around his neck, raised his hand and spoke up.

"Uhh . . . buy land?"

We all started laughing.

"Yeah, you're right," B-Jax said with a chuckle. "Technically you can't build a house unless you have some land. But let's just say you already own the land and you want to build a house . . . what's the first thing you have to do in order to build it?"

RJ surprisingly raised his hand and confidently gave his answer. "Put the foundation down."

B-Jax nodded his head. "Exactly. Exactly. Well, what's a foundation?"

Next, Polo decided to take a crack at it. His father laid concrete for a living and every weekend all summer he had his boys
out there with him. "It's like . . . it's what you put down first to
make sure the house doesn't fall."

B-Jax was proud of his answer. "Bingo! You set the foundation
first so the house doesn't fall. If there's a house built with a poor
foundation," B-Jax continued, "but it looks really nice on the outside, how long do you think the house is going to last?"

The entire circle unanimously shook their heads side to side.
It wouldn't last long.

"Don't matter what it looks like, Coach. That house is done
for!" Polo yelled out.

"Yup, you're right," B-Jax agreed. "It's not going to last very
long, huh? But now let me ask you this: What about a house
where the foundation is rock solid? You don't rush it, you spend
time on it. You make sure that foundation is perfect." At times,
B-Jax was part philosopher and part ball coach. He wore many
hats and he wore them well. I could see the light bulbs start to go
on in many of the young men standing before us. "Now all of a
sudden it doesn't matter what the house looks like on the outside.
As long as that foundation is set and strong, how long do you
think that's going to last?"

It went quiet. The message was being received. Tre Singleton
raised his hand and stepped forward. "Forever, Coach. It will last
forever."

"Thank you, Tre. You're right. *Forever*." B-Jax smiled. "That's
what we're trying to set right now. A foundation for this team, for
this school, and for your lives . . . that will last, forever."

5

QB1

RELISH IN THE GREATNESS AROUND YOU

What size? Green ones or black ones?"

The sparkling summer sunshine gleamed, the rays bouncing off my iconic Oregon Ducks football cleats. At Oregon we were known for our lightning-fast offense, but our flashy uniforms and first-class equipment were even more famous.

A single-file line of high-schoolers formed at the trunk of my old rusty Jeep. It's hard to play football in Converse and tennis shoes, so it was time for me to fix that. In college, I took the first-class equipment for granted. The University of Oregon football program was so well funded that we were given whatever we needed, whenever it was requested. The uniform combinations were unlimited, and each combo came with a pair of cleats. Green, yellow, black, white, chrome; my cleat collection was bigger than most people's shoe collection. Weekly, at every game, we were given a new set of cleats to ensure we looked good and played even better. After five years in the program, I had more cleats than I knew what to do with. After my playing days were over, I packaged them up in three giant trash bags and stashed them away in my mother's storage unit.

The smiles on the faces of my players shined as bright as the cleats I presented them with. Some players had football cleats of their own, but others couldn't afford them. For anyone who couldn't afford them, today was like Christmas.

"Alright, I got sizes ten and a half, eleven, and eleven and a half."

The only advantage to having a small number of players was that there was no chance I would run out of personal equipment to give to them. We only had thirty-five players and my cleat collection far exceeded that. As for the big guys that couldn't fit in my old playing shoes—I came prepared.

"Coach, I wear size thirteen though!"

I stored the bigger sizes in the front and back seat. Thankfully, I had the ultimate Nike plug. My big cousin Michael, who originally inspired me to take a leap of faith and go to Jesuit High School, had a career working for the shoe company at the World Headquarters in Beaverton, Oregon. Once he heard what I was doing for the students at Parkrose, he reached out and offered his help if I needed anything.

I took him up on that offer: *What's up Michael, can you get your hands on some cleats? Size 12 and up?*

He texted back, short and sweet. *You know it. I got you.*

As a ball coach, it's imperative you show your big boys some love. The offensive and defensive linemen at any level are always the unsung heroes of a football team. It takes smart, tough, and, most importantly, unselfish individuals to play in the trenches. Imagine playing an entire game or entire season and not getting an ounce of credit for the success of the team. Well, that's the life of a lineman. They do the necessary or "dirty" work. The quarterback, running backs, and receivers make the highlights, but no catch or run is made possible without the big boys up front who block and sacrifice for their teammates. Some of the best teammates I ever had the pleasure to play with were linemen. Being a team player is ingrained in the DNA of the position. I never overlooked the unsung heroes of a team, so naturally, I made sure every foot size was accounted for before I popped open the trunk to my Jeep. Nothing can beat the feeling of giving back to the kids, especially when there's a Nike swoosh or Oregon "O" attached to the gift.

Everyone in the program was finally equipped with the proper gear. No more tennis shoes on the football field. Another small win for the Broncos. The field work consisted of sprints and agility work, but we had yet to get on field with an actual ball. The group was starting to look like a team, but B-Jax and I still didn't know exactly what we were working with from a "football" standpoint. Could we run routes, catch, and throw? Did our guys know any fundamentals to the sport? All of that was still up in the air.

"Alright boys, two lines!" I hollered out as we got on the field after B-Jax's grueling weight room workout.

We had yet to decide on positions, offense and defense, and, of course, the starting quarterback. We knew who our group of offensive and defensive linemen would be. That part was easy; pinpoint your ten to fifteen biggest kids and there you have it, those are the linemen. The other positions on offense were a little more nuanced. And while every position on the field is important, it is fair to say your quarterback carries the greatest level of responsibility and impact on the game. Midway through our summer workouts and while interacting with the kids on a daily basis, we all agreed that Jay Jay would likely be the best fit for our starting quarterback. The position was up in the air since we handed out workout gear and cleats, but Jay Jay made a great case to be the man under center.

Jay Jay was the definition of a natural athlete. He was tall and lanky, standing at six foot one with a lean muscular build. On the very first day on the job, our athletic director raved about his athletic ability and potential, but after I saw him run with my own two eyes, I was blown away. Did he like running? No way. But was he talented and one of the fastest high-schoolers I had ever seen? Yes, without a doubt.

Beyond athletic ability, Jay Jay was as talented as they come. He lit up the room and made coaching this team a blast. Besides having an infectious personality, the dude could do it all: he could sing, dance, rap, draw, write, windmill dunk—you name it, and he could do it. Potential oozed out of him in every aspect of life.

"Two lines, one right here, and one over there." I gestured to the patch of grass to my right and left. It was difficult to instruct without painted lines on the field. I tossed Jay Jay the ball. "You got QB," I said.

Jay Jay was a tough read at times. On most days he was the light that drove our team's optimism. But on other days, he was down, and unmotivated or just flat-out missing. At first I couldn't put my finger on it. From the outside looking in, he seemed to have it all. But as I got to know him, it all started to make more sense.

Since a very young age, Jay Jay was the chosen one of his family. As a youth football player, he was a bona fide star. He was bigger, faster, stronger, and more agile than his counterparts. The things he used to do on the football field as a kid were special. And with every year that passed, the legend of Jay Jay grew. His family put pressure on him, tapping him as the one that was supposed to make it out and make it big. As he grew up, the pressure wore on him and made the sport he used to love less enjoyable. Just a year ago, he took the easy way out and quit. He was done with the pressure, the expectations, and the attention. Thankfully, he decided to give me and the new-look Broncos another chance.

Now, as a seventeen-year-old, Jay Jay had developed into a physical specimen. He was an explosive athlete with a rocket for an arm. With the flick of a wrist, he could throw a perfect spiral that cut through the air like a hot knife through butter. I wanted to use the quarterback to run the football, making quick zone-read decisions as a dual-threat option. Spread the field and let my QB go to work. Jay Jay fit the bill. He looked the part and had the physical tools to do it. But like nearly everything at Parkrose, things were never that simple.

Although our attendance had come a long way, we still had room for growth. There were kids like RJ and Tre that never missed a workout—not since that day when B-Jax and I had to round them up. But there were players that wanted nothing to do with our training. Some excuses were valid but most of the time I was getting played.

For as fast and athletic as Jay Jay was, he sure hated working out. Early in the summer it was an everyday struggle to get him to the weight room on time. Mornings would usually start with me asking the group of eager teenagers, "Where's Jay Jay?"

Like clockwork, Jay Jay would come moseying in a solid fifteen minutes after start time. With the wave of B-Jax's finger, Jay Jay would drop his bags and pay his one-mile debt before he joined the group. In fact, Jay Jay racked up so many late days and so many miles that midway through summer, he basically just stopped showing up. All of a sudden, he became like a solar eclipse, a rare sighting.

One afternoon, after another tardy morning by our quarterback, I pulled him aside to get to the bottom of it.

"Jay Jay, my guy, we have to figure this thing out. What do we have to do to get you here on time?" I was frustrated. I recently gave him the reins to our offense, and I needed Jay Jay to be a leader and an example for the rest of the team.

On schedule, he responded with his favorite excuse. "I know, Coach. But it's not my fault, it's the bus. I can't get here on time."

I thought about pointing out how he was able to get to school on time riding the same bus route during the school year, but I held back. I had another response locked and loaded, something any coach from my past would have said: *If you can't get here on time, then wake up earlier.*

Neither of those comments would have moved the needle in the direction we wanted to go. Our team needed their quarterback and it was ultimately my job to get him there.

"Listen, you have to stop with the excuses," I said. "Your teammates need you here and I need you to show up on time. I get that you've got issues getting here, but everyone on the team does. This isn't just your problem."

I tried to take him under my wing early, knowing if I could teach him the value of pushing past his comfort zone, his life could be changed. Jay Jay was a rare shining star at a place with very few bright spots. A year ago, he walked out of practice and never came back after a disagreement with a coach. I didn't want to be too hard on him and have history repeat itself, so I made sure to tread lightly.

"Yeah, I get it," he said. "But I'm not everybody else. I gotta catch two buses, then walk the rest of the way. It ain't easy, man."

I continued to preach. We needed to eliminate the excuses. Once you stop making excuses, you'll be surprised at what you can accomplish. No excuses, only action. So, I figured I'd help resolve the issue for him.

"Okay then, I'll swoop you up every day. Every morning." What could he say to that?

"Nah, you don't have to do all that—"

I cut him off. "No big deal at all. I'll pick you up."

Looking somewhat confused, but likely enjoying the notion of a free ride, he agreed. The very next morning I started my new route, driving twenty minutes east from Parkrose to go pick up my QB before our 9 A.M. workouts. After the workday was finished, I'd drop him back off. We did this every day for the rest of the summer.

Once the rest of my team caught wind that Jay Jay got rides every day, my car was never empty again. My beat-up Jeep seemed to always be filled to the brim with kids. Whether I was pulling into the PHS parking lot or out of it, the Jeep was full. The gas money hurt my pockets, but it got them home safe and kept them off the city bus. A fair trade-off.

One less thing to worry about, I always thought. But even then, there were bumps in the road. One morning, after a few weeks of perfect attendance, I showed up to Jay Jay's house, arriving there early enough to get us both to workouts on time. We spoke the night before, confirming that I'd be there at 8 A.M. ready to go. I woke up early and drove the twenty-minute route to his house and knocked on his door. To my surprise there was no answer. I retreated to my car and texted him. *I'm here.* Again, no response. I let a few minutes pass before I called. No answer. In a last-ditch effort, I knocked on the door one more time but there was only silence on the other side. I waited another fifteen minutes outside of his house trying to reach him. But he never answered and never came out. I got stood up by my quarterback.

Initially, it was heartbreaking. I'd gone above and beyond to help, and had it thrown right back in my face. By now, I knew Jay Jay well enough to know that he was most likely on the other side of the door waiting for me to leave. The next few days came and went without any signs of him. Our boys stayed the course, and B-Jax and I kept pressing forward.

Next Monday rolled around. To my surprise Jay Jay was waiting for me on the sidewalk outside of the gym doors, bright and early.

"Coach, can we talk for a minute?" he asked.

I was relieved to see him. His presence had been sorely missed during his one-week sabbatical. He was a great player, that went without saying, but his true value was his personality. If anyone could cut the tension with a well-timed joke, it was Jay Jay. His friends and teammates loved him. Those types of guys play a massive role in building the dynamics of a locker room.

"Of course, man. We missed you around here," I responded, taking a seat on the curb in front of us.

He joined me, also sitting down with his forearms resting on his knees. "I'm sorry, Coach. That one morning I messed up. I slept in, my alarm didn't go off. I should've just called you but I didn't."

Did I really believe he slept in? No chance. But he was man enough to come to me, face-to-face, and take some accountability. He apologized. That was more than enough for me. Life wasn't easy for him. From a young age he bounced around from house to house, never quite finding a stable living situation. At this moment, he was living with his uncle. From my understanding, it was a tough, no-bullshit household. Only Jay Jay actually knew what he was going through. The best I could do was try to understand.

I wanted to figure out why this outgoing kid with so much to offer to the world was so up and down. If he just stayed the course, football could be his avenue to jump-start his life, like it was for me. He was blessed with the talent most people dream of, but at times it seemed like he didn't care.

So, I asked him, point-blank. "Jay Jay, you're talented. I know you've heard it a million times, but you're the type of athlete college coaches look for. You have a real shot at playing at the next level. At times, when you show up, you look like you enjoy what we're doing. But most days you're here, I can tell you're not into it. So what's your *why*? Why do you play?"

I expected to hear the usual answer any seventeen-year-old would give: *"Because I want to play ball in college"* or *"Because I want to go to the NFL."* But Jay Jay was as smart as he was talented. He paused for a second and thought about it. I sat there next to him on the curb, just hoping to get the truth so I could learn a little bit more about him.

"To be honest, Coach, I know this is going to sound weird . . . but I don't even like football."

Not expecting that answer, I sat there in silence. I looked at his face and he was serious. Jay Jay was telling the truth.

"People my whole life tell me what I'm supposed to be and what I'm supposed to do. This game used to be fun back when I was young. But the older I got the more everyone around me tried to put me in a box. All anyone ever cares about is football this, and football that . . . that's why I quit last year. I had enough."

Hearing Jay Jay speak his truth, from the heart, hit me like a ton of bricks. The early pressure I put on him caused him to stop showing up. I anointed him the QB that was going to lead the school out of the depths of a twenty-three-game losing streak. Without realizing it, I put unwanted pressure on his shoulders. I was blinded by his talent on the field, making me no better than the people that weighed him down in the past.

In that moment, I thought about Jay Jay and his interactions with his teammates. When it was about football—the lifting, the running, the lectures by Coach Lowe and Coach Jackson—he was painfully disinterested. But in those moments where football wasn't the main focus, his true self shined through. Hanging out after workouts, cracking jokes in the locker room, dancing to the stereo in the weight room: in those moments Jay Jay could forget the pressure and expectations. It was now clear to me he didn't decide to come back this year because he liked playing football. He decided to come back because he wanted to be a part of a team.

After our curbside talk, the mutual respect grew. I understood where he was coming from and he understood I wanted the best for him. I now had an idea of what made him tick, but before we would close our conversation and head to workouts, I had one more question.

"You know you don't have to play football this year, right? If you don't like it, why put yourself through this?"

Jay Jay understood his impact on the football field and on his teammates. He sat back, shrugged his shoulders, and replied, "I want to help these guys win. We deserve it."

I left that conversation with Jay Jay with a better understanding of who he was. Every week I spent around these guys, I seemed to learn something new. In order to be the very best coach and leader for this team, I needed to take the time to have real conversations with them. Often, as adults, we think we know where the next generation stands because we were once in their shoes. But times change, and the world we live in transforms. The only way we can help our young people is by listening to them first. I assumed that Jay Jay Hudson, known as the best athlete in the school, automatically loved the sport he was playing, just like I did when I was his age. Thankfully, he gave me a chance to have a real conversation that shed insight into why he was the way he was. I became a better coach because my understanding of him grew. From that day forward, we kept our dialogue going. He would open up to me about certain things in his past, like some of the challenges he experienced at home, and I would do the same. And most important, we mutually agreed that he wouldn't be suiting up to be quarterback this fall.

To some degree, that was a hard pill to swallow. Now we were more than halfway through the summer with no quarterback. Positions were starting to work themselves out, but with no quarterback, our season would be doomed. We needed someone our guys could rally around. I looked at my team and decided I didn't need to choose the most physically qualified candidate to play QB, like I did with Jay Jay. I needed to choose the kid that I could trust to show up day in and day out. And there was no one more dedicated than Tre Singleton.

Originally, I had planned for Tre to play tight end for me. He looked like a tight end, standing six feet two with a big athletic frame. He was a great athlete but definitely more of a bruiser than a finesse player. His main position was middle linebacker.

He loved football for one reason and one reason only: he got to hit people. Now, having your starting middle linebacker double as your starting quarterback was an uncommon choice, but sometimes at Parkrose, nothing made sense.

In just a short time, Tre and I had come a long way. I trusted him and his dedication to what we were trying to build. Oddly enough, however, the first real conversation we shared was just after he had been in trouble with the law. It must have been the first or second week on the job when Mr. Shelton welcomed me into his office during my periodic lunch visit.

Drake sat down at his computer, in typical vice principal fashion, and started clicking the mouse and typing on the keyboard. "Coach Lowe, real quick. This weekend one of your players ran into a little bit of trouble. Nothing serious, but just wanted to fill you in."

This was the last thing I expected to hear during my second week on the job. "What happened? Everything alright?"

"Yeah, yeah, everything's okay. His name's Tre Singleton . . . not sure if you've met him yet. But anyway, this weekend him and a buddy broke into an office at an apartment complex. No one was arrested, and nothing was stolen, but they have Tre on camera. This situation shouldn't be an issue moving forward, I took care of it. Just know this kid's a little lost right now, Coach. Football is the only thing he's got and I would hate to see him throw it all away."

Ironically, the more teachers and staff warned me about a kid, the more interested I became in taking him under my wing. Mr. Shelton was an optimist. He believed in his football team and the young men that were on it. The conversations changed a little bit when I spoke to other members of the school staff. The reviews I collected about Tre were mostly positive, but I could tell their viewpoints were mostly based on potential.

"He's a really nice kid, but . . . ," one teacher began.

"He works hard, but he's just not a great student," another told me.

His teachers liked him as a kid, just not in the classroom. Well, I could work with that. Clearly, they had been around Tre longer than I had, so any information was useful information. One thing I did know, based on the incident at the apartment complex, was that he lacked good judgment.

I finally caught up with him a week after his run-in with law enforcement. "Alright Tre, let's talk some football," I said. It was a spring afternoon. I was fresh on the job. We walked over to the football field and leaned on the metal fence. "I heard about what happened this weekend."

As soon as the words came out of my mouth, he put his head down, clearly ashamed that I had already found out.

"But when things like that happen," I continued, "the most important thing is you man up and take responsibility for it, then you learn from it. Everyone makes dumb mistakes, but if you don't learn from those . . . then that's when even bigger mistakes happen. The kind of things that can *really* get you in trouble, if you know what I mean."

"Yeah, I feel you, Coach," he responded in a low tone. His eyes were glued to the ground.

Changing the tone, and the subject, I pointed out to the field in front of us. "You know, Tre . . . I learned when I was a kid, football can be more than just a game to play on Friday nights. It can be something that changes your life. It can be something that changes your mindset.

"The football field is an outlet. It's a place where you can go and nothing else matters. When you're going through something, let football be what takes you away from those things, even if it's just for a couple hours."

"All I want to do is play ball, Coach. That's the only thing that matters to me. It's the only thing that makes sense. I got so much shit going on outside of here . . ."

I sensed I was on the right track, giving him feedback that he needed to hear. "And that's what this game is, bro," I said. "It's our outlet. It's our way to balance out our lives. Now, the only thing we can't do is jeopardize that. We have to make the right choices off the field too. You feel me?"

It was a good start. I credit that conversation as the reason he stuck so close to me when we eventually started workouts. I wanted to hear his story because it was clear he didn't have much guidance. We concluded our talk by the field, and naturally I asked if he needed a ride home. Without hesitation he eagerly accepted.

We hopped on the freeway for a few miles and continued our conversation. He told me about his willingness to do whatever the team needed and his love for playing linebacker. I had just met the kid but he was already a joy to be around. He directed me through a few lights and turns from the freeway exit. Surprisingly, he guided me into a big parking lot shared by a Burger King, McDonald's, and a Broadway Inn.

"You can pull up right over here and I'll hop out," he instructed as I turned my silver Jeep into the giant parking lot.

"This is where you stay?" I asked. I couldn't believe it.

"Yeah, Coach," he responded innocently. "Just for now though. It's actually not that bad, it has a workout room."

Never in my life had my own personal problems felt so insignificant. I had so many questions for him, but the biggest one was clear: How did he end up living in a motel? That spring afternoon was a wake-up call. What I was doing was so much bigger than just football. Some of these kids really needed me.

The more Tre spoke, the more I realized he was wise beyond his years. Life will do that to you. He shared his story with me, how his parents suffered from substance-abuse problems ever since he could remember. As he went through elementary and middle school, he assumed their way of life was normal, because that was all he knew.

Just a year before, as a freshman in high school, his mother got sick and was admitted to the hospital. That same week, their family got an eviction notice. They were low on money and struggling. After the eviction his family moved to a temporary home for six months, just to get kicked out by the landlord again. Watching him tell his story gave me the chills. He was calm and casual. Reliving these moments seemed to have no effect on him. It was normal to him. He lived in the moment with no intention on looking backward.

After the second eviction, the family split up and his parents separated. One sister moved in with his aunt, the other moved in with her boyfriend, and his mom and dad went their respective ways to find a place to stay. Each place had just enough room for the members of his family but none of them had enough room for him. He got left in the dust with nowhere to go. As a freshman in high school, Tre Singleton was homeless.

I imagined being a fifteen-year-old on the streets. The fact that he was standing here today was impressive. Through his entire freshman year and a portion of his sophomore year, Tre bounced around from house to house. Some nights he would sleep in his sister's car, other nights he would find refuge in the heated stairwell of his friend's apartment building. Early on, no one at the school knew, until Mr. Shelton discovered why he was missing so much school as a freshman. And now, Tre was back with his father making it work at a motel.

As I sat in the car, listening to Tre's journey, half of me was truly heartbroken. But the other half felt inspired. And then it hit me. The kids I had the opportunity to work with were much more than they appeared to be. They were some of the toughest kids I would ever have a chance to meet. Unfortunately, Tre's story wasn't unique to the Parkrose experience. He wasn't the only homeless teenager at the school or on the football team. Some of these players were literally in survival mode. Most of them were dealt a difficult hand, to no fault of their own. Tre, especially, had every excuse to take the wrong path in life. He was fighting his fight, and I felt fortunate to be someone in his life that he could lean on.

Since that fateful day, it became my mission to teach this team that the struggles and circumstances they've encountered could make them tough. Many of the boys lived in situations that required them to be tough and resilient—they just didn't realize it because it was their normal, everyday life. As a coach or teacher, you often have the ability to see inside a young person and point out what they can't see themselves. Even so, I don't think we give our young people enough credit for living and fighting through challenges that they have no say in. When you're dealt a hand of cards, you have to figure out a way to make them work for you.

From that day forward Tre never missed a workout. He was all in. He embraced the daily grind and opened up to the messages Coach B-Jax and I were delivering. After hearing his background, my respect for the young man went through the roof. He was still prone to mistakes, but being a once homeless fifteen-year-old on the streets with parents who were struggling . . . I would say he'd done a damn good job for himself. He had earned my trust, outworked his teammates, and competed in the weight room and on the field.

As we ground through spring and summer, you could see the confidence within him grow. So, after Jay Jay and I had our discussion about stepping back from the quarterback position, it was a no-brainer who could lead this winless football team.

"Hey Tre, you ever played quarterback?"

"Quarterback?! No way. I can't really throw a football, but I used to play baseball."

"That's good enough. You're going to be QB1 this year."

Sometimes it's best to just rip off the Band-Aid, so I told him right there on the field, just like that. As soon as "QB" came out of my mouth, he cut me off.

"Whoa, whoa, whoa. Coach, you serious? I can't—"

I stopped him dead in his tracks. "You're fine. We're going to get you right. You're going to make history here, Tre. You're my guy, I believe in you."

He took a deep breath and accepted his destiny. "Yes, Coach. Like I said before, whatever I got to do to help the team . . . but one question . . . I'm still playing linebacker, right?"

"You kidding me?" I laughed. "Dude, you ain't coming off the field! You better get in shape, it's going to be a helluva year."

6

BAD NEWS BRONCOS

MOWING THE LAWNS AT PARKROSE HIGH

July was coming to an end, and the anticipation continued to build as we edged toward our first game. Local news outlets began to preview the season ahead of us, predicting the likelihood of yet another losing season at Parkrose. While playing college ball, I was never one to read anonymous comments underneath news articles. The majority of the time if someone has something to say, it's going to be negative, especially if their name isn't attached to it. But as a twenty-six-year-old first-time head coach, I couldn't help myself. I wanted to see what people were saying about me and my Parkrose Broncos. One anonymous poster, on an Oregon high school sports site, wrote the following:

> This was worth a shot by Parkrose. Coach Lowe's name recognition and playing reputation will give him instant credibility with those kids. There will be a bit of a honeymoon, but Coach is going to see some things he's NEVER

seen before, certainly not at Jesuit. Parkrose has had a season here or there over the past 40 years where they've had
a decent football team but this school has no real history
of success to build upon. Coach will be baffled when kids
miss practice and don't communicate, when kids walk
away and quit at the first sign of adversity, when they run
into academic and discipline problems which keep them
off the field. He'll soon realize how far from "home" he
is . . . I wish him luck and hope he isn't discouraged when
the reality of what he's signed up for sinks in.

It really pissed me off that someone took the time to construct
a paragraph about why I would fail. I immediately took a screenshot and stashed it away for future reference. It became clear how
people around the city felt about the Parkrose community. This
anonymous post was representative of that in a nutshell.

*No real history of success to build upon . . . Coach will be baffled
when kids miss practice and don't communicate . . . When kids walk
away and quit at the first sign of adversity . . . Academic and discipline
problems . . . Hope he isn't discouraged when the reality of what he's
signed up for sinks in.*

The words on the screen made me cringe. And to be honest,
they affected me more than I originally imagined they would. The
more negative comments I read, the more protective I grew over
my kids. The poster had embraced the stereotype of a kid from
Parkrose, loud and clear. I felt for them. Was there some truth
in the anonymous post? I would be lying if I said there wasn't.
But I also knew that kids have academic, discipline, and quitting
problems at every high school across the country. My team of
Black, white, Polynesian, and Mexican kids were easy targets, so it

was my job to protect them. Stereotypes are deeply embedded in the makeup of the world we live in, but honestly, you only really think about them when they affect you or people you care about. I cared about the kids being slandered online.

Most coaches would call this kind of stuff "billboard material," and post it in the locker room to rally the troops. The problem was that our community had been beaten down and overlooked for so long that these guys believed this was an accurate description of them. Showing them the comment would do more harm than help. It would likely be yet another kick when these kids were already down. Instead, I kept the screenshot for myself, reading it over and over. Each time, I faced the reality of how people saw us, which only motivated me to prove them wrong.

Heading into the last week of summer workouts, the waters were surprisingly calm around Parkrose. The team continued to show up ready to work without making excuses. Were we perfect? Not at all, but we were growing in the right direction. The wild card of the group was Polo. A big Polynesian kid, he was a natural. Our plan was to line him up on defense directly in front of the center and let him go hunt. You can't teach aggressiveness, and Polo just had it in him. He loved hitting people, a good recipe for a D-lineman.

Two of Polo's best friends, classmates, and rugby teammates were also Polynesian: the brothers Kobe and Lebron Roebeck. (I'm sure you can guess who they were named after.) Lebron, just a sophomore, was a tall and lean kid with long arms, obviously still growing into his body. Kobe was the opposite. He was a year older than his brother, but shorter and stockier. Their crew ate lunch together, played sports together after school, and went to church together on the weekends. Their families were close-knit, and from day one, they treated me like their own.

Polo was the ringleader, the tough guy of the bunch. After seeing what he was capable of in the weight room all summer, I wished I had a few more players built like him. Our team was made up of a bunch of tough but scrappy kids. As a whole, we were fast and athletic. But in terms of size, we were smaller than I would have liked.

During the last week of summer, Polo pulled me aside.

"Yo Lowe, I got a question."

"And I have an answer. What's up?"

"I got two more rugby teammates that want to come here and play with me, LeBron, and Kobe! They heard about what we were doing, Coach. They want to be Broncos."

My eyes lit up. "Do they live in the school district?" I asked him. It was the only question that mattered.

"Yessir," Polo replied. Music to my ears.

"Alright, tell your boys we would be happy to have them. If their parents want to talk, feel free to give them my number. I'll talk to Drake to make sure we can get them enrolled the right way and answer any questions they might have. After that we'll get them started."

"Aight . . . good!" Polo cheered, with a smile on his face. "I was hoping you'd say that!" Then he laughed and smacked me on the shoulder. "Because I already told them they were good. They'll be here on Monday!"

And just like that, the family got a little bigger.

Vice Principal Drake Shelton did his due diligence and agreed to let them enroll and join the team. It felt like an overnight miracle.

We had them on the practice field in no time. They still had to clear some red tape before they could get equipment and strap it up with us for the first practice, but we felt a sense of comfort seeing those two rugby players looking on.

One of them, Ricky, we happily referred to as Big Rick. Ricky was built like a brick house, only five foot nine but weighing in at 250 pounds. He would anchor both our offensive and defensive lines. Mile (Mee-Lay) was the other, a big solid athlete that had exceptionally quick feet, especially for his size. Those two, along with Polo, were part of our "large and in charge" Polynesian family. They joined Kobe on the offensive line, solidifying a sense of protection for our quarterback and running backs. They all made it clear, however, that football was their second sport. These boys weren't just your average linemen, though. Rugby requires everyone on the field to be able to catch and run with the ball in their hands. So naturally, these boys had quick feet, soft hands, and unassuming speed. The presence of Big Rick and Mile added another level of confidence to our program.

Though he was a welcome addition, Mile didn't come alone. He brought his little sidekick with him wherever he went: his nine-year-old brother, Sione. Everywhere Mile went, Sione was seen traveling closely behind. Mile and Sione come from a family, a lot like mine, where it's all-hands-on-deck. Everyone has to pull their weight around the house in order to make things work.

During the summer, I would learn, it was Mile's responsibility to babysit little Sione. They were inseparable and clearly had that special brother connection. Seeing those two walk up to the practice field every day brought back similar memories of me and my younger brother. Just like me at his age, Mile was responsible for his younger sibling and he took his job seriously. If Sione needed to be picked up after school, Mile would drive over to the elementary school, pick him up, and drive back for practice. He didn't always make it to practice in time, but that was okay. He handled his business and I admired his hustle. During practice, Sione became my unofficial assistant coach. The kid wanted to be around football, but more importantly, he wanted to be around his big brother. We all chipped in during practice, every coach on staff, making sure we kept an eye on young Sione so Mile could do what he loved.

After the final treacherous week of hard work and grueling workouts, I gave the kids a week off before we strapped on the helmet and pads for the first time. We battled through the summer workouts, and they were finally complete. It was the calm before the storm. Things were going to get really busy, really quick.

It was finally time to strap on the helmets for the first time. It was a good feeling—there's nothing better than the first day you get to put the pads on. It made you feel like a warrior, ready to face anything in your path. Now, these warriors had mismatched gear, different-colored pants, a rainbow of helmets, and anything we could bootstrap together to ensure they were at least safe to play ball. But frankly, they didn't care. They worked hard to get to this point, and mismatched practice gear was all they had ever known. For me, as a former Oregon Duck with ten different helmets and thirty different uniforms, it was quite the sight. But we weren't looking to win any beauty contests. We just wanted to play ball.

Entering an official first practice as a first-time head coach was nothing like entering it as a player. As a player, you have a certain excitement and adrenaline. All you have to focus on is yourself. Your job is to make sure you know what you're doing and that you're prepared to do it to the best of your ability. As a head coach, I had those same butterflies in my stomach and adrenaline flowing through my veins, but instead of worrying only about myself, I had to focus on not messing things up for the *entire team*. It's a different type of pressure, planning and executing a practice structure that makes sense and hits all the areas that a football team needs to improve. I had stayed up late each night during our off-week, organizing each day of practice to ensure I was giving our guys the best chance to succeed. I became obsessed. I loved what I was doing and who I was doing it with.

I had a full staff by the time practice number one rolled around. It was no longer just B-Jax, security guard Brian Alves, and me. We were joined by another former University of Oregon teammate, Mike Garrity, who believed in me and my vision. After walking on to play linebacker for the Ducks, he went on to earn a scholarship because of his competitive spirit and willingness to do whatever the team needed. I always respected the way he carried himself as a teammate. The best thing about former teammates is that you can always count on them, as if you're still playing side by side. B-Jax and Mike perfectly exemplified that. They believed in what I was doing, so they were willing to help. Mike was a ball coach by nature. Like me, he had an obsession for the game and saw coaching as his calling.

After a few informal interviews I also decided to hire two young aspiring coaches, Blake and Spencer, that lived in the neighborhood. They had never coached a day of football in their lives, but they were eager to learn and I could get down with that. Spencer, a few years younger than me, was an alumnus of Parkrose. He knew the school and community inside and out, but more importantly, he had firsthand experience as a student in that building. It was important to bring in someone who had once walked those halls. Although neither Blake nor Spencer knew how to coach, it was important to give more young dudes an opportunity to help out the community.

A counselor, Marty Williams, rounded out the staff. From the first week on the job, Marty welcomed me with open arms. I spent those first couple of weeks at Parkrose learning how the school operated on a day-to-day basis. Marty introduced me to Elevate Oregon, a program designed to increase learning and college readiness at schools in the area that need extra support. Marty was part of a hardworking team that oversaw our students to make sure they stayed on track and were given the resources they needed in order to succeed. Because of Elevate Oregon, and the skilled counselors working it, every student had a chance to graduate. They were creating opportunities to succeed during and after high school. It was clear Marty had a great relationship with the students, so I welcomed his Parkrose expertise.

When you compared our boys to our coaching staff, there were a lot of fitting similarities. Our staff was filled with young coaches, all different shapes, sizes, and colors. As a staff, we were just as mismatched and dysfunctional as our students at times. Just a bunch of prideful young coaches trying to figure it out, often butting heads behind closed doors. We were a confident bunch and wanted the best for the kids, but we all had one common characteristic: we wanted to win.

I planned each day and each practice meticulously going into our Fall Camp, our full-gear practices in August leading up to our first game. Finally, after all we'd been through, we made it to the real thing: helmets, shoulder pads, and tackling.

Just months ago, I was hanging up flyers in the hallways and begging kids to come out and play, but now, we had weathered the storm. It was time to play ball. Each and every day of camp was carefully curated to teach these kids discipline, build confidence, and, of course, work on our football skills. But life had other plans. No matter how much I planned, there was always something that was going to turn the master plan into shit.

Our stadium and football field were a lot like our weight room: outdated and in need of a face-lift. We were the only school in the entire city that still had a grass game field. Over the last ten years, Portland-area high schools raised money and got special funding from the state to update and install turf fields. Unfortunately, our school was forgotten, and it was just too expensive to replace our field with turf. Grass meant intense upkeep. Leading into our practice week, I called the maintenance staff to ensure the field would be ready on the date of our first practice. The overgrown and disheveled field needed a good cut and chalk lining, as the previous year's field markers had faded through the seasons. I coordinated the dates, gave them a practice calendar, and thanked them on behalf of our program. It would be nearly impossible to teach football without fresh-cut grass or markers on the field. The maintenance folks registered my request: "Yeah, sure. We got you, no problem, Coach. We'll make sure the grass is cut. We'll make sure the lines are painted." At times it felt like I was doing everything by myself to give my kids a chance, so it felt good to know the maintenance crew was there to support us in our quest to break the losing streak.

Day one of Fall Camp rolled around, the practice plan was set, and all the coaches were fired up. The staff showed up on the first day an hour early to review the practice plan and prep for the big day. But as we walked into the arena and our eyes landed on the field, we immediately recognized a big problem: the grass was two feet tall, full of wild weeds, and there were no lines on the field. Another "here we go again" moment. My first reaction was straight panic, then anger. These maintenance guys lied to my face. They let us down. How could I be so foolish to believe that those guys would have my back? Still shocked, I started to think about that anonymous post from the article I had read earlier in the week. That guy wasn't kidding. Parkrose was full of surprise after surprise. If this school was going to break the losing mentality that had cursed it for so long, we would need the support of the school and community.

The losing mentality was a curse throughout the school, not just in our kids but also in many of the staff members who worked there. People online thought we were losers, and it was clear even people in our own building felt the same way. No one thought we had a chance, not even the maintenance workers. I imagined their conversations in my head: "Why would we go through the trouble of lining the field and cutting the grass if they're going to lose every game again?"

An hour before my first practice as a head coach, we didn't even have a proper field to practice on. Curveball after curveball. If nothing else, at Parkrose you learn to adapt, and you learn to adapt quick. As a head coach your job is to deliver the message to your team. All summer my message was clear: *We don't make excuses.*

Being a head coach forces you to look within yourself, and to live what you're preaching. After the initial shock at the realization that even the maintenance crew wasn't on my side, I got my shit together and figured it out. No excuses. I brought the coaches into a huddle and started to direct. We had a little less than an hour to salvage the day, and that's exactly what we were going to do.

"Alright. Alves, you got the keys to the maintenance garage, right? Go get the lawn mower and drive it out here."

"Mike, you go get the chalk. It's over there in the football shed."

"Spencer, you and Blake follow Alves to the garage, grab the two rakes. I think there's a leaf blower in there as well, that might help too."

When things don't go your way, the only solution is to adapt. You can always choose to make the best of your circumstances, and on that day, that's exactly what we did. We marched down the field in an assembly line racing against the clock. One coach drove the lawn mower from sideline to sideline. Behind him, another coach moved the freshly cut grass to the edges of the field with a leaf blower. After the blower, the two rakes fell in line, raking up the missed pieces of grass into small piles on the sideline to ensure the chalk had direct access to the freshly groomed ground.

To finish it off, Coach Garrity followed with a small pushcart that drops chalk as you push it forward, creating the coveted lines we needed. After an hour, when practice was supposed to start, we were drenched in sweat and had only managed to cut and line fifty yards' worth of football field. The kids showed up to practice, watching from the side as their coaches furiously cut, lined, and raked the field. It was certainly something to see. They looked on, some laughing and others offering to help. It was just another hectic day at Parkrose High School, but something special happened as the kids watched in their mismatched gear. They saw firsthand that their coaches were dedicated to them. That we were willing to do anything for them in order to give them a fair chance to win. As B-Jax often said, "Actions speak louder than words." We not only talked about being a family but we treated them like one too. We were committed to the kids that made the choice to dedicate themselves to us. We were willing to do anything for them, even if that meant cutting the damn grass on our own.

After salvaging our football field on the first day of camp, it was finally time to get to work. Our team was a jigsaw puzzle of sorts, and our mismatched uniforms were a perfect symbol of our mismatched positions. My main objective was to figure out where all my players fit in. To the outsiders we were still the Bad News Broncos of old, but we knew the truth. We were a close-knit group that expected good things to happen because we put the time in.

Kids with different-colored helmets, jerseys, and pants. Coaches who all looked like they were fresh out of college. And a football field with fifty yards' worth of crooked lines. This job was a constant test, and from the outside looking in, it must've been a pretty funny sight. Without the maintenance guys in our corner, we had to accept that we weren't practicing on a field with football lines anytime soon. No sidelines, no hash marks, and no numbers. Offensive football, a lot like basketball, is a game of spacing. Alignments and depths are critical to learning the game and installing an offense.

After a week's worth of attrition to the field, the lines slowly faded away into nothing. We accepted the fact that we would have to teach the boys how to line up and run plays on a literal blank patch of grass. The fiasco of cutting the grass and painting the lines just wasn't worth it anymore. By now, we were used to making the best out of any situation, so that's what we did.

I wanted our kids to do well, and these boys deserved it. The motivation was there. They were sick of being the laughingstock of the school district. They wanted some respect, and so did I. The kids had survived the spring and summer seasons, but a week into camp, things were picking up steam. We had thirty kids in our program, down from the forty-five that we originally started with. The ones that stuck it out and embraced the shift in culture, those were the ones I was ready to go to battle with.

But, like most things Parkrose-related, there was always another surprise in store. RJ, who always seemed to be up and down, continued to struggle. He was, by far, the most complete athlete we had on our team. Football was easy for him. He could run, he could catch, and he was as tough as nails between the lines. But regardless of how talented you are, if your attitude is poor and inconsistent, it doesn't matter how fast you can run or how high you can jump. By now I had a pretty good read on him. I knew he was fighting a battle from within so I always offered a helping hand in any way I could.

He would have a week or two of great practices and then suddenly, without any signs or warning, he would snap. It had been a roller-coaster relationship, but I cared greatly for the kid and I wasn't willing to give up on him. I would let things slide, but I also had to reel him in when things got out of hand. Eventually, though, we hit a breaking point.

Two weeks before our first game, RJ pushed it too far and forced my hand. A shouting match broke out between RJ and Coach Mike Garrity at practice that week. That wasn't anything out of the ordinary. RJ didn't care for Mike, and I think the feeling was mutual.

"Alright, you're out!" Garrity screamed, motioning him to

leave the drill. "If you aren't going to listen, then we'll get some-one else in that will!"

But RJ, to my dismay, refused to come out. Coach Garrity caught RJ on the wrong day, and it got out of control quickly. The two shouted at each other, the coach telling the player to get out of the drill and the player refusing to do so. We were two weeks out from our first game and we looked like a disaster: a coach and a player arguing in the middle of the field while the entire team looked on. We needed to focus and prepare for the game. Distractions wouldn't be helpful, so I had to do what I could to eliminate them.

I walked over to try and put out the fire. "What are we do-ing? We're wasting time! RJ, listen to your coach. And Mike, calm down, we're good."

If RJ wasn't already upset, I must have put him overboard. Now he felt backed into a corner so he turned it up a level. It got bad, quickly. He yelled and cussed us out, completely losing con-trol. It wasn't the first time I saw him lash out, so I knew it could definitely get worse.

He started to walk off the field and violently ripped off his helmet as the rest of the team looked on. Uh-oh—I knew what was coming next.

"RJ, stop!" I pleaded. "Don't do it!"

He held his helmet by its face mask and cocked his arm back like a pitcher on the mound. He stopped midmotion and looked me in the eyes. I yelled again from across the field.

"Don't do it!"

He froze and, in an instant, made his decision. He reached back with helmet in hand, swung his arm forward as if throwing a discus, and launched his helmet thirty yards across our field. Everyone went silent. We couldn't believe the level of disrespect.

"Get out! You're done!" I said, pointing to the locker room as RJ walked off the field, proud of what he had just done.

Our uphill battle seemed to be getting steeper and steeper. This job was not for the faint of heart. You had to be willing to endure the obstacles and adjust on the fly to unexpected moments like RJ's outburst.

Like usual, RJ showed up the next day at practice as if nothing happened. That was his style, and quite frankly, I did him no favors by allowing it in the past. He expected everyone to have short-term memory as it related to his behavior. He verbally battled me after not showing up to workouts, he threw the punch at B-Jax, and overall, he had been a selfish teammate. But enough was enough. It was no longer about giving him a chance to be part of a winning team. The stakes were higher. Now, I needed to intervene to save his life. Teachers and coaches had tried to correct his behavior with every method in the book. Every method except one.

Before practice, the day after the tantrum, he was on the sideline stretching in full gear, helmet and all. I knew I had to do what was best for him. I walked up to RJ and pulled him to the side and asked him in a straightforward and calm voice, "What are you doing here?"

"I'm . . . I'm ready to practice," he responded, in a quiet, shaky tone.

I looked at him, and while it broke my heart, I had to deliver the news. "You're done, RJ, you're not a part of this team anymore. What you're doing is affecting everyone. Your actions are hurting the team and regardless if you wanted it or not, your teammates look up to you. I was counting on you to be a leader for these guys."

I would be lying if I said my heart wasn't racing in that moment. It hurt to deliver that message to a kid I genuinely cared about. But if I wanted to make a real difference in his life, I had to step up and do what was best for him. I was expecting an epic war of words and emotion, but to my surprise he accepted his fate. He pushed back a little, but ultimately, he knew he was out of line for what he did the day before. It was time to make a point: sometimes you don't realize you need to change until something you love is taken away from you.

After the tough conversation, RJ went back into the locker room and took his gear off. As we started the day's practice, now without one of our best players, I saw RJ out of the corner of my eye marching up the bleacher stairs. He sat and watched practice from the top row. The next day, he returned to the same spot on the top row of the bleachers and watched as his teammates prepared for their first game.

As the days went by, RJ finally started to understand what it felt like to be held accountable. For the first time in his life there were consequences for his actions. It hurt to see him up there in the bleachers by himself. B-Jax and I had put so much energy and attention into showing him there were people out there that wanted the best for him. We gave him chance after chance, yet neither of us seemed to get through to him. We had to make it clear to RJ that playing sports is a privilege and that it can be taken away if you aren't doing the right things. It was a hard lesson to learn, but an important one. We weren't going to let one bad apple spoil all of our hard work. As we completed the last week of camp before heading into game week, our group remained small yet committed.

It was crazy to think how far we had come. The kids were coming together, committed to winning and snapping Parkrose's twenty-three-game losing streak. They didn't want to be the laughingstock of the Portland high school football association, and the only way to change the minds of our competition would be to beat them.

A week away from the start of the season, it felt like I had already played one. Most days I was gassed out by the time I made it back home. This team was putting me through the wringer. Every day had been a fight, but I was determined to make this thing work. By the start of camp, I had quit my job vacuuming floors and setting up rooms at the MAC club in the early mornings. Mr. Shelton continued to check in and press me about the security job that would be available in January. Between the roller coaster of coaching this team and the early morning grind at the MAC, I figured I needed a change. So, I did the math, calculating how much money I'd have to subtract from my savings account to survive the months until the start of my new job working security at Parkrose. That five-thousand-dollar stipend check I received for coaching ball proved to be more important than I originally thought. Money would be tight this season, but I was determined to cut some of my expenses and make it work. Coaching this team was now my full-time job. It was almost like I was back in the NFL coaching—except for the paycheck, of course.

To celebrate the dedication of the Broncos, I decided to open my small home up to my thirty players. With the help of the other coaches, we planned a team barbecue. I invited my family:

my mom, girlfriend, brother, and close relatives. I even decided to invite my dad, the best chef I knew, hoping he would come through for me. It had been a rocky road over the last ten years, but football always connected us. I was so proud to have my own team, so naturally I wanted my family around to meet them. Me and my dad always had a good relationship. Since I was a child, I was always realistic with my expectations of him. I knew he battled demons, so I never took offense if he didn't show up for me. There were times he wouldn't call me back when I called, other times he would flake out on plans. The worst was when he would go missing for weeks or months at a time. But nonetheless, I made it a point to always be his lifeline, and his doorway back to his family. Regardless of any lack of communication, I made sure he would always know he had a bridge back to us. People in his life would turn on him, but me, his son, I would always have his back.

That's why I dialed his number. After one ring, the voice on the other end of the phone answered with excitement. "What's up, kid!"

Dad didn't always answer so I was relieved to hear his voice. "Not much," I said. "Doing my thing, chasing around these kids. It's been a wild ride."

"Parkrose is no joke. I know you're doing it the right way. Stay at it and good things will happen. You got any kids that can play?"

"Wait till you see. I got some dawgs, I'm tellin' you! I got a little running back named Taydrian, that little dude can run! My QB is a beast, about six-two, he plays linebacker too. And wait until you see this D-lineman I have, Polo . . ." These kids drove me crazy at times, but I sure was proud of them.

It had been a while since Dad and I last talked. I got so excited that I almost forgot the reason I called. I got back on track. "Anyways, I was wondering if you could help me out," I said.

"Anything, kid. What you need?"

"I'm having a barbecue at the house this Saturday. I could use your help setting it up, helping me throw down on the grill. You know, like the old days."

As soon as the words left my mouth my dad was all in. "You got it! What kind of meat you cooking? Dogs and burgers are always good for a big group. Let's do some chicken breast. I got you on the grill, let me do the cooking so you can make sure your kids don't burn the house down!"

And just like that, my dad was in. He helped me plan the party, pick up the meat for the grill, and even came over early to prep with me. On a hot and humid Saturday afternoon, the kids began to trickle into my backyard as Dad manned the grill. My mom and big sister ran around, helping me set up for the thirty teenagers. My younger brother set up the TV in the backyard and hooked up the PlayStation to it. It was a special moment and a special scene for me. The Lowe family was back together for an afternoon barbecue, and the Parkrose Broncos football team could enjoy the reward for all their hard work. I had put in a great deal of effort to keep both together. Both families were a little broken at times, neither of them perfect, but both perfect enough for me.

As perfect as it was, it wouldn't be a Parkrose event if there wasn't something unexpected. This team may not have won any football games in the past three years, but they were a tough and scrappy bunch. One of the players had brought over a couple pairs of boxing gloves. While my dad and I were inside cleaning up after the kids' feast, I heard the sound of loud cheering and hollering coming from the backyard. I peeled back the curtains and looked out the window to see a wall of kids outside, in a large circle surrounding two kids in the middle wearing boxing gloves. It looked like a scene out of *Fight Club*. The crowd cheered on the fighters as they threw jabs and hooks. These dudes always had a surprise up their sleeve.

I sprinted outside and jumped in the middle of the circle while simultaneously hearing "BOOO! Let them fight!" from the crowd. Sure, they were having a great time, but I couldn't help but think about what the school administration would say if they caught wind that Coach Lowe was hosting boxing matches at his team cookout.

"Ayy Coach," Polo yelled. "It's no head shots, we're good! No head shots!" It was a funny moment, one that actually gave me great pride even though I had to throw in the towel. We clearly had a lot of fight in us. I hoped it would show on the football field, not just in the ring.

The barbecue brought the boys closer together. Up to that point, they had done everything I had asked of them. Sure, there were bumps in the road, but perfection was never the expectation. I simply expected each and every player to show up, work hard, and cut the excuses. I was happy to say, a week out from our first game, our kids had taken that message to heart. We still didn't know what it felt like to play on a real football field with lines, hash marks, and pylons, but we would just have to cross that bridge when we got there.

We showed up for practice on Monday. It was game week, and time to focus the kids on our first live competition as a reborn program. We had been prepping for months. We knew what plays to run, who needed to be where on defense, and who the starters would be. Tre Singleton and Taydrian Jackson would be in the backfield as our QB and RB, respectively. Jay Jay was ready to go at wide receiver. Our offensive line group was made up of Big Rick, Mile, and Kobe. And of course, our enforcer, Polo, was revved up and ready to hit anybody from the fullback and defensive line position. I didn't know how we would perform, but I knew there wasn't much more we could do to prepare.

For the first time ever, this group of players started to feel as if they had a chance to win. One of the best feelings in the world was seeing my boys start to walk and talk with more and more confidence. They believed in themselves, and they believed in me. The level of comradery we built at practice was clear. Kids cheered each other on, high-fiving and chest-bumping. The level of competitiveness we practiced with was admirable: guys hitting each other and then helping each other up. They were becoming a team, and you could feel it and see it in everything they did. They knew they could succeed; they could win. When I recall my high school football days, game day remains my favorite part of my playing career. Nothing is better than those Friday night lights.

The game was scheduled for Friday at 7 P.M., and we had just concluded our Thursday practice. I gathered the kids around me in a circle on the field, this time without boxing gloves.

"Take a knee, fellas."

Almost in rhythmic motion, the guys all fell to one knee. Some because I asked it of them, others because they were ready to collapse anyway. As I surveyed the kids, I couldn't help but feel a sense of satisfaction. We had come so far, even though our official journey had hardly begun.

"You guys ready? I got those first-game jitters already! I'm so excited for y'all. Even now, people always ask me, 'What were your best football memories?' Or 'What was the most fun? Where was your favorite place to play?' I've been around a little bit and played in some big games, but I'll always say, and I will say it forever, that my best football memories came from high school. It came from doing exactly what you guys are doing right now.

"Win or lose, we show up, put in the work, and we don't make excuses. That's who we are and that's what we do. To trust and rely on one another and to leave it all on the field. The lights, the cheerleaders, the smell of football in the air. You are about to experience it. This field is where you grow. It's in between these lines where you learn the most about yourself."

I paused for a second. "Look around, man. Look at your teammates." The boys, on bended knees, turned their heads side to side, and looked at each other. "We've been through so much already. Regardless of what happens tomorrow, the people in this circle, the people on this field, will have your back. You go out there and fight for each other. Battle for your brothers. Tomorrow there's no more mismatched jerseys. No more mismatched helmets . . . Tomorrow, we show up to the fight, as one!"

The kids jumped to their feet and started hopping up and down. They were no longer thirty mismatched kids from different backgrounds and different upbringings. There was no black, white, or brown. For the first time in their high school careers, we were all one thing and one thing only—Broncos.

Big Rick stood in the middle of the circle and yelled, "Everybody up on me!"

The team huddled together, surrounding Ricky, in the middle of the field with their hands in the air.

"Bad Ass Broncos, on me, Bad Ass Broncos, on three! *One! Two! Three!*"

And with great pride, my once overlooked and underappreciated team yelled out together in unison: *"BAD ASS BRONCOS!!!"*

7

COMMITMENT DAY

JUST DIAL THE NUMBER

Scoot back! Scoot back!" I yelled and pleaded from the sideline. We had made it, the first play in the first game of my head coaching career.

"You're offsides! Get back!" I begged.

Unfortunately, my voice fell on deaf ears. Moments earlier, I sent the play in as the Parkrose offense was huddled up, ready to start the new season off right. Tre, in his first ever game at QB, called the play and they broke the huddle. This was our first time playing on a real football field with turf, hash marks, and lines. As we broke the huddle and ran to our formation, my wide receiver, Tony, ran to the first white stripe he saw. The only problem was that the ball, or line of scrimmage, was two yards behind the white line where Tony planted his feet.

Every coach on the sideline yelled and waved their arms frantically but little Tony was locked in and in the zone. Tre took his place under center.

"Ready . . . set . . . go!"

The second we snapped the ball, yellow penalty flags flew in the air, and the high-pitched referee whistle blew the play dead. *Offsides, Parkrose.* Our first play of the season was a dud.

During the week I played out every possible situation in my head, but a penalty *before* the first play was something that hadn't crossed my mind. It wasn't Tony's fault.

If proper planning prepares you for success, then I really screwed things up far before that first yellow penalty flag. Our first game was in Vancouver, Washington, against Prairie High School. Although we played ball in Oregon, and Prairie played in Washington, our schools were only a twenty-five-minute drive from each other, Portland being in northern Oregon and Vancouver being in southern Washington. Both cities were right at the state border. It was a quick drive over the Columbia River, which split the two states.

We were scheduled to kick off at 7 P.M., and I clearly didn't plan ahead well enough. Coaching and teaching were the fun parts. Those are the things you think about when you take over a high school program. It's the other responsibilities that often don't cross your mind until it's too late.

In my head, leaving two hours before kickoff was the right thing to do. I did the math, not wanting to get to Vancouver too early, but at the same time knowing we needed to get there with enough time to get off the bus, go to the locker room to suit up, and get warmed up on the field to ease into the game. Well, at least that was the plan. What can I say? I was young and confident. By the time the first game came around, I thought I had it all figured out. All I had to do was get my kids to the game so they could have their shot at redemption. Easier said than done.

When 5 P.M. rolled around, my kids were accounted for, everyone had their gear, and we loaded up the necessary game-day equipment. After double-checking the necessities and taking one last head count, we hit the road in our yellow bus right on time with two hours until game time.

What started off as a twenty-five-minute drive across the Columbia River toward Vancouver quickly turned into a long and painful marathon. It was smooth sailing until we hit the freeway, where we encountered bumper-to-bumper traffic with a line of cars as far as the eye could see. On a normal weekday, it was an easy drive with little obstacles, but this wasn't a normal day. It was Friday at rush hour. I sat in the front of the bus helplessly watching the minutes tick by as we moved foot by foot in that yellow bus.

The clock read 5:45 P.M. when my phone buzzed with a text from our athletic director, Daunte, who was already on-site.

Where you guys at? You getting close?

I pulled up the GPS app on my phone and typed in the location, hoping I would have positive news for Daunte. I popped in the location and desperately waited for my phone to respond. In a matter of seconds, I got my answer. The GPS calculated our arrival time: 6:20 P.M.—thirty-five minutes to our destination.

My stomach dropped. I really screwed this one up. The forty minutes before kickoff didn't even account for the time it would take for all my kids to get their things off the bus, get into the locker room, and put on their pads and shoes. It was terrible planning, and I had no one to blame but myself. I felt bad that this was how we were starting the new season, but most of all, I was ashamed and embarrassed. It was kind of ironic how all summer I taught my kids about the importance of being on time to your obligations.

When a player would show up late and make an excuse I always responded by telling them to plan out their mornings better—leave earlier so you get to workouts on time.

In a way, I had just as much to learn as my boys. Being responsible for thirty kids and a handful of coaches is a different type of pressure. The football part was fun, and that came easy. The scheduling, the team meals, the fundraising, and the logistics had a steeper learning curve. That moment, as I sat on the bus praying for the traffic to let up, I learned a painful yet positive personal lesson: I was not immune to mistakes, regardless of how prepared I thought I was.

We pulled up to the stadium thirty minutes before the scheduled kickoff. My assistant coaches scrambled to get everything off the bus and my boys sprinted into the locker room to get dressed and back out for warm-ups. Ideally, before games you would like to be calm and focused. Well, because I didn't get us there on time, my coaches and players were the furthest thing from calm and focused. If you weren't sweating from the hot bus ride, you were sweating from running around pregame like a chicken with its head cut off.

While B-Jax and the assistants helped get the players into the locker room and out on the field, I walked over to meet the opposing head coach and referees. I tried to appear cool and collected as I walked over, so they'd think I was unfazed by the bus debacle. But on the inside, I had that extreme feeling of shame and embarrassment.

We all shook hands and exchanged introductions, but before anyone said a word, I blurted out, "I apologize, guys. We hit more traffic than expected."

The Prairie High coach seemed to be a good guy and offered

us some much-needed help. Clearly, he and the refs had made a plan before we arrived. "Don't worry about it, Coach. Do you want to delay the start of the game? I think we can give you guys about twenty more minutes on the clock and we can kick this thing off at seven twenty. Sound good?" He looked over to the refs for their approval and received a head nod in agreement.

Surprised at what I just heard, I accepted. "That would be fantastic. We would appreciate that."

Maybe the opposing head coach was just a really good dude. Or maybe they scheduled Parkrose High School for their first game for a reason, presuming this would be their warm-up game. Either way, they threw us a bone and we gladly accepted it.

We used every second of our extra time up until kickoff at 7:20 P.M., but we still found ourselves yelling to let Tony know he was offsides on the first play of the game. With the hectic situation I put them through, I couldn't be surprised about how the game started. We weren't ready to play. Or maybe I just wasn't ready to coach. That surely wasn't how I envisioned the first play of my head coaching career. Needless to say, we weren't off to a great start.

I stood on the sideline, fighting through the self-doubt that came over me as the referee signaled and called the penalty.

"Offsides, Parkrose—five-yard penalty—first down."

The referee picked up the ball and marched back five yards. Our guys huddled back up and waited for the real first play of the game. Tre ran over to me and I communicated the play, hoping they'd line up in a straight formation this time. Although I was still drowning in my own self-misery, I stopped to take in and appreciate the special atmosphere of the Friday night lights. The stadium was much bigger than the rinky-dink one we had at our school. The smell of hot dogs and burgers was in the air and the sounds of the opposing school's fight song echoed alongside their band. Our stands were much smaller, but parents, administrators, and classmates showed up to support our boys. I would be lying if I said I wasn't a little nervous. If I was nervous, I could only imagine how my boys felt.

Our offense lined up in a spread formation. Tre loudly said, *"Ready . . . set . . . go!"* The center snapped the ball. Tre caught the snap and handed it to our running back, Taydrian. Before I could blink, Taydrian dodged a tackle and turned on the jets, running down the sideline before getting pushed out of bounds for a fifteen-yard gain. Our sideline erupted with cheers.

"Let's go, Tay!"

On paper, we matched up well with the Prairie football team. They had a few kids that could really run, and a few that were big bodies, but so did we. They were a formidable opponent, but from the looks of it we had a chance. The biggest difference, though, was the number of players they had on their sideline. They were a much more established program and it showed by the amount of kids who wanted to play ball over there. After another first down, and a couple great efforts by Taydrian, our drive stalled and we were forced to punt.

Our defense was finally up: Polo Moeaki time. Number 44 trotted on the field after the change of possession. Behind him, our starting quarterback, who doubled as our starting middle linebacker, followed. On offense, it takes a little bit more thinking, which can lead you to play slow. Every football coach in America will tell you: *The more you think, the slower you play.* So being able to watch my team play defense was a different experience. They were able to cut it loose a little more, and not think too much.

Thinking and reacting are not exclusive to either side of the ball, but generally, there's more thinking on offense and more reacting on defense. There's a little more freedom that comes when you play defense.

The Bronco defense came out on fire. Polo smacked around the opposing team's offensive line, and Tre flew around laying big hits on the ball carriers. We gave up a few first downs, then buckled up our chinstraps and made a huge stop near our end zone to get the ball back. After a few back-and-forth defensive stops, the score was 0–0 heading into the last few minutes of the first quarter. Although I figuratively dropped the ball earlier in the evening, we were still competing and in the fight.

On defense you get to play a little more freely, but sometimes that bites you in the butt. It was the tail end of the first quarter in a defensive battle. They were driving on us, but our kids were holding strong, getting stops, and making tackles. Defensive football is more reactive than anything else, but if you react to the wrong place, the opposing offense can make a big play. That's why offenses move people around pre-snap, send them in motion, or shift. On offense, they are always trying to get you out of position by drawing your eyes to the wrong spot.

Their offense, with fifteen yards to go to score a touchdown, called the play and lined up in their formation. The quarterback screamed out, *"Ready . . . ,"* as he started his cadence. He lifted his foot off the ground, communicating with his receiver to run toward him. As soon as that foot lifted off the ground, the receiver took off like a rocket toward the QB.

Tre yelled out, "Motion! Motion!" while tracking the receiver on the run.

"Set . . . go!" The center snapped the ball just before the

receiver ran behind him. The QB caught the snap, then stuck the ball in the stomach of his full-speed receiver. Tre's job, as a linebacker, was to *read* and *react*. Unfortunately, in the moment, he read and reacted to the wrong thing.

As quick as the QB flashed the ball in the stomach of his receiver, he pulled it back out. The receiver ran hunched over as if he was carrying the football. Tre read the play and reacted to what he saw. They tricked me too, watching from the sideline. As Tre and Polo reacted to the man without the ball, a giant gap opened up in the middle of the defense. The hole parted like the Red Sea and their QB sprinted into the end zone untouched from fifteen yards out. *Touchdown*. They kicked the extra point and the score was now 7–0 at the end of the first quarter.

The start of the second quarter didn't quite go our way either. Only being down seven points, we felt pretty good about our performance thus far, but things spiraled out of control quickly. After a turnover, Prairie got the ball back and marched it right down the core of the defense. Maybe they finally got their early game jitters out or had finally figured us out. Either way, when they got the ball back, we couldn't stop them. They threw it, ran it, and were clicking on all cylinders.

They marched down the field in an impressive drive to go up 14–0. My kids were down but, from the look of their faces on the sideline, we were far from out. They encouraged each other and picked themselves up off the ground. We had worked so hard to become resilient. Being down a couple touchdowns wasn't going to faze them. We got the ball back with the intention to go down the field and punch one in.

Before the offense went out on the field, I gathered them around for a quick message. "Alright, boys! This is a big drive.

Focus on your job, execute your assignment, and take care of that football! Its's that simple, keep fighting, boys!"

It was only the second quarter, but it had already been a long night for the Broncos offense. We tallied up a few first downs but still didn't have anything to show for it. We needed a big play so I tried to create one. Tre had come a long way since the day I told him he would be playing QB for us. Every day he was growing and getting more confident in himself. But when it came to throwing the football he wasn't where we needed him to be. The kid had a strong arm, that was never the problem. The problem was in his head. He was an overthinker.

I understood where he was coming from. Tre wanted to be perfect. But on the way to perfection there are inevitably going to be growing pains. In practice, instead of simply letting the ball fly, he would often overthink the throw, causing him to either sail the ball long or leave it short. It was something he was working through, and who could blame him? He had never played a day of QB in his life until he met me.

We broke the huddle from the sideline. Up until that point, every play I called was a run play. We were down, but still in striking distance. Needing a big play, I figured it was time to give Tre a shot. We put Jay Jay back in at wide receiver for the pass play. The best athlete on the field was on our team, so why not throw it up to him and see what happens.

I sent the play in and the boys broke the huddle. The play was designed to hit Jay Jay on a deep post down the field. No one on the other team could run with him. Frankly, I doubt there was anyone in the entire state who could run with him. The boys lined up in formation and Tre called the cadence.

"*Set . . . go!*"

Kobe snapped the ball. Tre caught the snap, and Jay Jay was shot out of a cannon. Watching him glide across the field was a treat. I just wished he was running like that with the football in his hands.

As soon as Tre dropped back, their outside linebacker blitzed off the edge, running full speed with a head of steam on Tre's backside.

We all screamed from the sideline. "Throw it! Throw it!"

He had Jay Jay running open in the middle of the field. Tre reached back like he was going to let it fly, but hesitated, holding the ball an extra second. In football, things happen fast. That moment of hesitation was just long enough for the blitzing linebacker to reach his destination. Tre didn't even see him.

CRACK!!!

The sound of the pads popped and echoed through the entire stadium. The opposing crowd cheered and the Parkrose faithful let out a cringeworthy *"OOOOHH!!!"*

I've been around ball a long time, and hadn't seen many hits like this one. Tre's body folded around the blindside shot he took in. Simultaneously, the ball flew straight up in the air. *Fumble!*

The Prairie defense would recover and celebrate by running off the field to chest-bump teammates and coaches while the Broncos peeled our QB off the ground. We were demoralized— not just the players, but coaches too. To make matters worse, on the very next play, the other team threw a bomb to a streaking receiver down the field. *Touchdown.* And just like that, we were down 20–0 in the second quarter.

During the final few minutes of the second quarter all any of us could think was, *We have to get to halftime.* The game was getting out of hand. We had to stop the bleeding. In football, you get some pretty funny bounces sometimes. We were backed up by our own end zone with just over a minute left in the half. The clock would run out if we just ran the football, so that's exactly what we did. If we kept possession of it, we'd make it to halftime without giving up another touchdown. Tre snapped the football, gave the ball to our sure-handed running back, who only fumbled it away for another turnover. When it rains, it pours. Three plays later, Prairie walked in for a touchdown just before halftime, taking a 27–0 lead.

Though we started better than expected, the only thought on my mind as I walked into the locker room was that our first half as a team was a complete failure. My head started spinning. I looked around at all the disappointed faces and couldn't help but accept that they weren't prepared to play because of me, their head coach. The negative thoughts came pouring in. *What did I get myself into? Am I really this bad of a coach? I can't even get my team to our game on time.*

We got back in the locker room, bruised and beat down, both mentally and physically. I've been through many wins and many losses, but never had I been solely responsible for an entire team. This feeling was different. It was that deep feeling of disappointment when you let down someone you care about, except magnified because I hadn't just let one person down.

As I stood by the locker room doorway, clearly reeling in deep thought, someone walked up to me and put their arm around my shoulder. It was my assistant coach, Mike Garrity. Now, Coach Garrity and I had been to war together many times before, back in our Oregon Ducks days. We've won and lost at the highest level of college football, but he knew this one was especially hard on me. Teammates are forever; when your teammate is down, it's your duty to lift them up. Coach Garrity took it upon himself to pick me up. Or slap some sense into me, actually.

"K-Lowe, don't forget, we got your back," Garrity said as the team was finding a seat in the cramped visitor's locker room. "Just remember, don't take this thing so serious," he continued. "We had a shitty half, so what? The halftime message to give to our guys is: How are we going to respond? That goes for you too, Coach."

People that truly have your back will always tell you the truth. He was right. Garrity laughed and nudged me on the shoulder. "Because I know damn well if you get hit in the mouth you're not going to stay on the ground, are you?"

That's what I needed to hear. Life is 10 percent what happens to you, and 90 percent how you respond. I had never been one to feel sorry for myself, but I'm human. Sometimes, you need someone to look out for you and simply tell you: *I have your back*. As I was doubting myself and searching for an inspirational message for these kids, my old teammate, now known as Coach Garrity, came through for me.

After a reality check from Garrity, I was back to myself. I put the bus situation behind me and focused on the young warriors that were sitting in front of me. I rallied the boys in the locker room with a heartfelt version of what Coach Garrity said to me. I wasn't going to let these kids give up on themselves, and the coaching staff I assembled sure as heck wasn't going to give up on them either.

We took the field in the second half with purpose. Our team stuck by each other, and they had each other's backs. We continued to struggle on offense. We had playmakers, but we just couldn't put everything together multiple plays in a row. Defensively, we played hard, and we played confidently. We showed toughness I hadn't seen before. Ultimately, we gave up one touchdown in the second half but didn't put any points on the scoreboard, losing the game 33–0.

In years past, a game that started the way this one did would have ended with a worse final score. We had good moments, and we had bad moments, but most importantly, for the first time as a team, we faced adversity and collectively decided to fight it. It's a choice whether or not you push through challenges or run the other way. And I was proud to see our boys show the signs of growth.

Still, I took the loss harder than anyone. I put my boys in a deficit before the game even started. The poor first half was solely on me. Whether you're a kid or an adult, there's always room for growth. This one hurt so much because I wanted our kids to know what it felt like to win. They should have had the opportunity to experience the joy of victory and the hard-earned fruits of their labor. The streak went from twenty-three losses in a row to twenty-four. At the end of the day, I had to coach better and figure out a way to get my boys ready to play . . . starting with getting them to the game on time.

As we drove back to Parkrose, the bus was completely quiet. The kids didn't have much to say. The silence showed me they cared. They believed they could win football games. Twenty-four games in a row, they'd had that same feeling of walking off the field, defeated by their opponent, but I could tell they had turned a corner. Like me, they hated the feeling of losing and they never wanted to feel that way again. Once losing bothers you, you will do everything it takes, every single time, to win. That was a lesson I learned at a young age. While I was fortunate enough to win a whole lot more than I lost, it didn't change my overall feelings toward not getting the job done, especially as a Parkrose Bronco.

A few years before, I remember being in the same shoes as my players. As a high school player, I had a career run. I played running back, wide receiver, and defensive back, and excelled at all three. As the Defensive Player of the Year in Oregon, I was selected as one of the top one hundred players in the country to play in the 2010 US Army All-American Bowl. Plenty of colleges came knocking on my door, all willing to offer me an opportunity to play ball for them. But as a young kid, I grew up watching one team and one team only—the Oregon Ducks. Ever since I could remember, I wanted to wear the green and yellow.

When Oregon came calling, when I was a junior in high school, it was a bit of a letdown. The head coach at the time, Chip Kelly, sought to recruit me as a defensive back and not a receiver. I never had anything against playing defense, I just didn't like being told what I could or couldn't do. Oregon wasn't the only school to say I was better suited to play defense. At five-nine, they weren't entirely off. But I had heart, knew how to find space, and, most importantly, I had speed. As a teenager I was quietly confident yet hardheaded. The more colleges that told me I couldn't play receiver, the more I convinced myself that I was going to do it. But my stubbornness overcame my desire to fulfill my childhood dream and play for the Ducks. If they didn't want me as a receiver, then I didn't want to go there.

I played out my senior season at Jesuit High School and ultimately decided I was going to play ball for Coach Steve Sarkisian at the University of Washington. They were going to let me pick my position, so I was all in. When it was all said and done, I earned the right to call myself an All-American and the opportunity to play in the Army All-American game at the Alamodome in San Antonio, Texas.

In San Antonio, I had the pleasure of rooming with Curtis White, a big burly tight end from Eugene, Oregon, who was all set to play for the hometown Ducks after graduation. We got to know each other, talked about the different routes we took, and ended up becoming friends. I complained about being slotted as a defensive back, and told him I would love to play wide receiver alongside him at Oregon.

Curtis was a straightforward dude, so he offered me some great, blunt advice. "I don't know, man, why don't you just call Chip and ask?"

"I can't just call him out of the blue," I said. "I haven't talked to him since junior year of high school. Besides, they don't want me to play receiver at Oregon."

"Maybe things have changed . . . The only way you'll ever know for sure is if you ask him, bro."

It's funny to look back at your life and pinpoint the forks in the road where you could have went right, but decided to turn left. If the All-American game never matched up Curtis and me, who knows if I would have had the courage to make that call. And he was right, it's best not to leave things in the "what-if" category of your life. Sometimes the only thing you have to do is ask. So I picked up the phone and called Chip Kelly.

After a few rings he picked up. "Hello?"

"Hey, Coach. It's Keanon Lowe from Jesuit High School. We haven't talked in a while—"

He cut me off. "Keanon . . . what's up, my man? Good to hear from you. How you been? How can I help?"

I hesitated, still unsure how to approach the topic. "Well . . .

uh . . . I know you are aware I'm headed to play ball at Washington. You know, the reason I did that is because I want to play receiver. I'm committed to the position and that's where I see myself. But . . . I just can't help to think what it would be like to play for you in that offense. I know you guys want me to play defensive back there, but is there any chance you have a scholarship for me at wideout?"

I paused, anxious for his response, somewhat scared he might laugh me off the conversation. But then, in typical Chip Kelly style, he offered a nonchalant, "no big deal" sort of response.

"Yeah. Of course we do," he said. "If you want to come here, we'll let you play wideout, I think our receivers coach, Coach Frost, will really like you. You had a helluva senior season. Our deal is, we want good football players and good people. We think you're both.

"Let's set up an official visit when you get back from San Antonio. We'll get you and your mom out here, and if you like us and end up picking us, we would love to have you."

We ended up going on a visit the following weekend and the rest is history. On signing day, in front of my best friends and family, I fulfilled my childhood dream by officially earning that full-ride scholarship to play for the Oregon Ducks.

I later learned that Chip gave me the shot because he knew I would do whatever it took to get on the field, regardless of what position I was playing. He recognized my true desire to be a part of his program. And as a hometown kid, he knew the Oregon Ducks program meant a little bit more to me than the other recruits from across the country.

I wanted to instill that same attitude and desire into my Parkrose team. If I was willing to put the work in, I'm sure Chip assumed that I could eventually get on the field at receiver. I would have to put the extra time in because I wasn't the biggest guy at that position, but he knew if I cared enough about it, I would find a way. High school football taught me a crucial lesson about believing in myself, even if someone says you can't do something. You must be willing to do whatever it takes to make it possible, but first you must never stop believing in yourself.

My kids were still in the early phases of figuring that out. The losing streak was now at twenty-four and we had a decision to make. Do we continue to believe in ourselves and commit to doing everything it will take to break the streak? Or do we give up and fold, and make excuses, like years past? It was time to see what we were made of.

8

THE "PROGRAM"

YOU GET WHAT YOU PUT INTO IT

Coach Chip Kelly wasn't a yeller, but he also wasn't the type of guy to back off an opportunity to push his team and his players to the brink. You could tell how much he thought of you by how much he rode you. He was especially agitated on a particularly dreary winter day in Eugene, Oregon. He was running by my side, shuffling his feet to keep up, and practically chasing me down as I booked it down the field.

"Faster, Lowe."

"Go. Move your ass. That's not good enough!"

"You keep moving like that and you won't ever play a down at Oregon."

"You think you've arrived? You're a long way from Jesuit. I need more from you! It's not supposed to be easy, Lowe. Go. Go. Go!!!"

Over the past hour of off-season workouts, Coach Kelly followed me around from drill to drill, yelling at me, pushing me, laying into me. It wasn't a particularly pleasant experience, especially because it seemed like he was picking on me alone, for whatever reason. Until my arrival at Oregon, I was always one of the best players, if not the best, on the field. The quickest. The fastest. The best hands. I was a stat-monster in high school, grabbing touchdowns and interceptions, stockpiling more than a thousand yards each year. I found a way to dominate every game. Now, for the first time in my life, I couldn't even sniff the field. As a redshirt freshman, I wasn't able to play in the games. I could only practice with the team. That was common for many first-year players, giving them the opportunity to further learn the game and physically develop without sacrificing one of their years of eligibility.

I arrived at Oregon feeling pretty good about myself. I was a top 100 player in the country, a high school All-American. And so I arrived on campus excited to play ball. But it quickly hit me that college football was an entirely different game. Compared to most of my college teammates, I was a scrawny eighteen-year-old, hardly a burger over 160 pounds. I wasn't necessarily small for a high school football player, but I walked into the Ducks' program and quickly realized that I had work to do. The speed of the game, the level of competition, and the talent you're surrounded by takes some getting used to. It takes a level of mental and physical maturity to play as a true freshman in a big-time college program. Admittedly, I didn't have it.

So, in many ways, I felt like I had to start over, and that's essentially what a lot of freshmen have to do. It wasn't easy to come to terms with the fact that I was going to have to sit out an entire season, taking all the hits in practice, sacrificing everything I could, but never see the playing field for at least a year. While

I would help the team get ready for games, I spent a lot of time that first year getting my face beat in and getting bullied and pushed around on the football field. At the University of Oregon, it was sink or swim.

It was all very new and humbling to me. I had earned a rightful place on that team, was a Division I scholarship athlete, and like many I went in thinking it was going to be a great year filled with highlights and plenty of touchdown dances. And then reality hit. The days were long and grueling, like working two jobs with no end in sight. A normal day consisted of waking up at the crack of dawn, dragging yourself out of bed, going to meetings at the team facility, then practicing for a few hours. After your first practice of the day, you'd often book it to campus for class, then to tutoring appointments to ensure you were making the grades to stay on the team, then back to the facility for more meetings. It was a brutal schedule.

The life of an NCAA athlete isn't easy. And on top of that, redshirts didn't even get to suit up for the game. That was a hard pill to swallow. You work your butt off during the week, fight through the injuries and the schedule of a student athlete, just so you can play. That makes it all worthwhile. It is the reward for all the hard work. Putting on your uniform, running through that tunnel, and hearing the thousands of people in the stadium cheer for you as you catch a touchdown. That moment is worth the sacrifice. It's a fair trade-off. But when you are redshirting, you practice your butt off, get beat up all week, and then on Saturdays stand on the sideline in sweatpants and a hoodie while waving a towel to the crowd. And that was the extent of our game-day experience. The grind was real. But as a freshman you had to take your lumps and keep moving, or else you got left behind.

But even so, I learned a lot of valuable lessons that first year. I woke up each and every single day and put in the work. I didn't become a star, or even a starter overnight. I had to chip away at it. With each practice, I pushed the boulder closer to the top of the mountain. I was stronger, faster, more adept to succeed at a higher level. The game began to slow down for me, and I could feel that I was beginning to find my sweet spot. It was overwhelming at first. But eventually things began to click. That said, it still took a great deal of patience. God, did I want to play. To be on the field, run the routes, catch a touchdown. Accomplishing dreams I'd had as a kid.

I learned that your goals don't just happen overnight. No matter how good you are, it's not going to come easy. Anything worth a shit or worth achieving takes dedication. And I knew that from the outset, but this was on a whole 'nother level because my identity up to that point was based on the fact that I was a football player. I'd been working on this dream of being a Duck since I was eight years old, so that whole year was a whirlwind as I realized things weren't going to come easy. I would have to dig deep in order to even play a few snaps at some point.

We had an unbelievable team that first year. Some of our starters were all-time Oregon Football greats like LaMichael James, Kenjon Barner, Jeff Maehl, and Spencer Paysinger. These guys were the real deal. Coach Chip Kelly had the program humming. Phil Knight and Nike were in the background, making the Oregon Ducks a national brand. The program was filled with stars and legendary coaches, and it was no accident we went on to run the table and win the Pac-10 Conference. That season, we went undefeated and played in the 2011 BCS National Championship Game. It was a weird dynamic for us freshmen, especially the ones that were waving towels on Saturdays. We were on a wild roller coaster riding the wave of the team's success. I walked into a situation, and before I knew it, we were undefeated and playing for a national title in Glendale, Arizona, against Cam Newton and the Auburn Tigers. We fell short in the title game, losing by a field goal, but the experience was truly remarkable.

I was surrounded with such high achievers on the football field and had no choice but to catch up or get the heck out of the program. After losing the title game, we went into winter conditioning. For whatever reason, mostly because I was young and dumb, I missed a few "optional" or "discretionary" workouts. I had yet to figure out what "optional" really meant in college football. I was naive, and even after one whole season I still hadn't figured out what it would take to touch the field.

After a week of optional workouts, I returned to the facility for circuit day. Circuit day was the most intense day of the week, focused on intense high-interval training. We split into groups of ten players and rotated stations every three minutes. At each station, a position coach would be waiting with his individual drill designed to gas you out until you quit. It was an unpleasant experience on any given day. But I arrived at the workout after a few days off, which meant it would be worse for me. I had a debt to pay to the coaches, and Chip was on my ass. As soon as the whistle blew, he started in on me.

"You think you can show up whenever you want? You want to do things your way? No. You do this our way." Coach Kelly proceeded to lay into me and follow me around as if I was the only one at the workout. Station by station, he stayed by my side, absolutely ripping me for what seemed like hours.

My brain was telling my body that I need to give up. And I'll never forget it. Halfway through the drills, I was huffing and puffing, about to throw up, and Chip got a foot away from my face. "You'll never play a down at the University of Oregon!" he yelled.

I was really shook. My head coach was telling me, to my face, that I was never going to play. Right then and there, he gave me an ultimatum. That day I went back to my college dorm room and did some real soul-searching.

Wow, am I really about this? I wondered to myself. *Do I really want this? What am I doing?*

I had to choose whether I wanted to buy into the program and be all in, or sit back and be satisfied with being on a team that went to the National Championship Game while I sat on the sidelines. Looking in the mirror and being honest with myself, I knew I wanted more for myself and for my college football career. His challenge snapped me out of my funk and recalibrated my work ethic, increasing my desire to be a Duck. Sometimes all you need is to have someone you trust tell you the truth. In that moment, Coach Kelly gave me a choice. He looked me in my eyes and said, "You'll never play a down at the University of Oregon." I knew he was telling me the truth.

I made the personal decision to buy in and do every single thing my coaches asked of me. As the days went by, I started building momentum and took that momentum into my redshirt freshman year, where I was able to earn playing time on special teams. I was always the smallest guy on the kickoff team, but they put me right in the middle because I showed no fear. I was willing to take any hit as long as I was on the field. I didn't care if I played one play a game or fifty plays. I was willing to do anything that helped the team, which was very much a part of the Ducks culture. And it finally clicked for me that, as a player on a team, it's your duty to dedicate yourself to do anything to help your team win, whether you're a starter or you're last on the bench. I carved out a small yet important role for myself that year as we went on to beat Russell Wilson and the Wisconsin Badgers to become 2012 Rose Bowl Champions. It was another special season with a memorable outcome, but I wanted more.

The expectations for the Ducks were sky high entering the 2012–2013 season. A handful of previous years' starters returned, but we were mostly a batch of unknown players looking to continue the legacy Coach Kelly was building with his Oregon teams. Our starting quarterback was a young dual-threat QB from Hawaii—Marcus Mariota—who would go on to win the Heisman Trophy and be drafted with the second pick in the 2015 NFL Draft. There was a certain attitude about that team. We knew we were good, ready to take the leap and do something special. As you could imagine, I wanted to be on the field as part of the narrative.

The mantra was simple: Win the Day. But even more fundamental than that was the way our coaches trained us to play. Three more words that were plastered all over the shiny Oregon facility: FAST, HARD, FINISH. Those three words were ingrained in my very existence. They would become my playing style, as well as the credo for all ninety of us in the program. Every practice, every game, every snap of the football—it was *Fast, Hard, Finish*. If you couldn't play fast and hard while finishing every rep in practice, Coach wasn't going to put you on the field. It was a simple equation that took me three years to figure out. Once I cracked the code, I took my opportunity and ran with it.

Going into Fall Camp of my sophomore year, there were a bunch of receivers vying for the same starting role for which I was competing. The local papers kept writing about those receivers, which I took personally. I was immersed in a culture of winning.

At the University of Oregon, everything we did was full throttle. We trained, practiced, and played harder and faster than the other teams in the country at the time. I knew exactly how I was going to climb the depth chart and earn my starting spot. I didn't like that I was being overlooked. I had a chip on my shoulder. The culture in our program was that the best players would play—no politics, no bullshit. If you wanted to get on the field, you had to work for it, and that's what I did.

I had spent my freshman year redshirting and getting the shit kicked out of me in practice, and then spent the next year scratching and clawing my way to a role on special teams. As we transitioned into my third season, which was my sophomore season of eligibility, I ultimately ended up going into Fall Camp and earning a starting spot as a wide receiver. My hard work finally paid off. It was my time. I battled my way through stiff competition with the other wide receivers. Ten guys competing for three starting spots.

When I stepped onto campus as an eighteen-year-old, I started an uphill fight to touch the playing field. Three years later, mostly filled with hard lessons and adversity, I found myself at the top of the depth chart as a starting receiver at the University of Oregon playing alongside our star QB Mariota, and other nationally recognized talents like De'Anthony Thomas, Josh Huff, Kyle Long, and Kenjon Barner. I was finally on the stage where I had always wanted to be. We entered the season nationally ranked in the top five with Coach Chip Kelly at the helm.

My official starting debut was in the first week of the 2012 NCAA football season, under the bright lights of Autzen Stadium in Eugene, Oregon. That game, the first of many, was the beginning of the rest of my life. My receivers coach at the time, Coach Frost, constantly spoke about taking advantage of your opportunities.

I took that message to heart, as did the rest of the team. Our Ducks team would go on to a 12–1 record, losing only to Stanford. After a successful season, we were picked to play in the BCS Fiesta Bowl, my first ever bowl game as a starter.

I learned, during that run at Oregon, the true value of buying in, remaining dedicated, and giving it your all. It was an important lesson, because I was at a crossroads at that time. Unsure whether I wanted to continue playing football at Oregon or just give up, Coach Kelly gave me the out. But I refused to take it. I knew I could play at that level, but I had to be willing to work for it.

And then there I was, six years later as a coach at Parkrose, with a team who just got crushed for the twenty-fourth time in a row. They were unsure of themselves, down and out, and I wasn't exactly sure what to expect back at practice the Monday after our game. I thought a lot about what I was going to say to get their spirits up, and approached the situation with a great deal of accountability. After all, I was in charge of putting them in the best situation possible to have the best chance to succeed, and the truth is I did a lousy job coaching my first game. Any good coach is always going to say it like it is, so on Monday before practice I stood in front of my team and told them how I saw it.

"Boys, this one's on me," I said as I looked at my guys on bended knees in the middle of the dead, yellow Parkrose grass. "We talked about having each other's backs, all summer, and since the day I stepped foot in that auditorium . . . I want to say I appreciate you for having my back on Friday night."

My team sat there in silence with looks of confusion on their faces. They were prepared for a typical verbal beatdown after suffering another historic loss. Instead, they got an apology.

"I got outcoached and they out-prepared us. That's on me, fellas. You boys had my back, you kept fighting and you kept battling. I will do better for you guys, you have my word."

As the words cut through the air, my guys sat there nodding their heads in agreement. Like always, I was calculated in the words I spoke to them. By design, the weight of the loss was almost immediately lifted as I delivered my message. As the head coach, it's always on you if your team doesn't perform well, regardless of the circumstance. I knew exactly what they needed to hear after yet another painful loss. Over the weekend I looked in the mirror, just like I did in those early practices at Oregon, realizing that I had to do better for my kids. Accountability was not only necessary for the players, but for myself as well. Although I took the loss especially hard, I still believed in myself and in my team.

They could do this. They had the fight in them, and I just needed to help them get it out. Most kids their age didn't have to experience the things they were going through. These were resilient kids, many of them homeless, hungry, and poor, with a natural chip on their shoulders. They were the toughest bunch of kids I had ever been around, but downfalls and struggles were simply normal to them. I could see things inside of this team that they hadn't seen in themselves yet. I knew that their daily struggles, the cards they were dealt, could be used to their personal advantage. I could see the toughness and resiliency inside each and every one of them. My ongoing mission was to open their eyes so they could see it for themselves.

I had just spent a Friday night watching my small group of kids take a physical beating up and down the field. But through it all, one concept stood out: every time we got physically knocked down, we got right back up. We weren't the biggest nor were we the fastest, but to say my team wasn't physically tough would be a bald-faced lie. For years, they'd been taking a beating on the football field and for the most part they kept coming back.

Where we were lacking was in the mental toughness department. When all you know is losses, in competition and life, it can wear you down, especially when you're just a kid. My boys were beat down mentally, no doubt about it. Last Friday night, I saw the glimmer of hope in the second half. Without them consciously realizing it, they collectively banded together and decided to stay in the fight. At any point in the second half they could have folded like in years past, but they didn't. I was proud to see that small step forward and looked at it as a building block.

When you're down and out, it's easy to let doubt set in and to ultimately give up. When adversity strikes, the natural human reaction is to feel sorry for yourself. At certain points in my life I've fallen victim to that simply because it's the easy way out. As their coach and mentor, I sought to make my team realize that adversity can be flipped into an advantage. There is no greater teacher in life than hard times. My kids at Parkrose had an advantage over everyone they were going to play against. That advantage was that they were real-life battle-tested. Whether they knew it or not, every day they were beating the odds. When it came down to it, all thirty players on the Parkrose football team were living in some form of tough circumstance that took a level of tenacity to get through. Not only were they learning to fight on the football field; they were learning how to fight in life.

At their core they were resilient, or else they would have quit a long time ago. My message was clear: It's okay to be different. It's okay to go through struggles in life. Just because they took an "L" doesn't mean they're losers. The circumstances they were born into don't have to define them. We all have the ability to make a choice to battle and to fight for what we want. So that was my message for the entire week. We were capable of beating the odds, in life and on the football field. Toughness is a mindset, and ultimately toughness is a choice.

All week I pushed that message. Chasing my players around the field, yelling encouragement as they transitioned from drill to drill: "Make the choice for yourselves! Never let anyone tell you what you're capable of! You decide, WE decide!"

I reverted back to the lessons I learned while helping raise my younger brother. Constantly pumping confidence and affirming that positive things will happen if you work for them: "You get out what you put in! Keep stacking good days and I guarantee good things will start to happen!" By now, the Parkrose football team was used to it. If you continue to push a message toward young people, eventually they will start to believe it. "We're the toughest team in the state! Nobody goes through the shit you go through! Every day you wake up, you battle!"

Day after day, I consciously reminded myself that these boys needed me, now more than ever. They needed the positivity. Most importantly, they needed someone to believe in them.

By the time game day came around, my boys were back on track. The kids were loose, excited, and ready to play. We were heading into our home-opening game against Benson High School. Like us, they were a perennial losing school with a small enrollment and little resources. This game would be a fair fight. By all means it was our best chance to get a win this season.

As we got closer and closer to the start of the game, I couldn't help but feel a sense of excitement. Like I was back in college, gearing up to play in the Fiesta Bowl. Although I wasn't buckling up a chinstrap anymore, the pregame butterflies were still the same.

There was a buzz around this game, and the bleachers were packed with our fans and family members. The Parkrose student body filed into the unkept football stadium by the dozens.

It was probably the biggest game at Parkrose in the past decade. Even with a loss already on our record, the entire community was still so excited to see what our new program had in store. You could feel the nervous energy in the locker room. I gathered the kids for one last message before we would take the field in search of our first win in three years. The silence was deafening, even though the muffled sounds of the school band faintly crept through the locker room walls. I looked at my boys, all thirty of them scrunched together in the small room. Some sat on benches and others leaned up against the lockers. They had a look in their eye, a look of ultimate confidence.

"Everybody take a deep breath," I said, the words directed at my boys. In reality, I was talking to myself as well. "Everything that's going to happen tonight on that field, you guys have earned it. You've done everything I've ever asked of you. Tonight, we turn the page. I don't care if a single person in that stadium believes it or not . . . it's not about them. It's about us!"

Almost simultaneously the butterflies and nervous energy in that room turned into adrenaline.

"Don't ever let anyone tell you what you're capable of! YOU decide that for yourselves! I wouldn't want to be anywhere else right now than right here with this team. Tonight, go out there and earn it! Win. The. Day!" As my voiced cracked and echoed against the cement walls, my boys matched my energy. We lined up two by two, eager to take the field as one.

"Win. The. Day."

As Coach Kelly wove in and out of ninety-plus players lying on the warm Oregon turf stretching, he continued saying it.

"We only have one choice if we want to be the best versions of ourselves. Win. The. Day."

Chip, the proverbial teacher, taught many lessons. But one, more than any other, stood out. He reminded each of us, again and again, that the best you can do as an individual and as a football team is to win the day. Do that, and you'll find yourself headed in the direction of your true goals and aspirations. After a third straight season with Chip, and a fourth consecutive BCS bowl game, Coach Kelly gained national attention and the eye of the NFL. After running all over Kansas State, the number-five ranked team, in the Fiesta Bowl, Kelly called a meeting as we all returned to Eugene after our break. It was odd timing for an impromptu meeting, so we immediately knew something was up. Normally, this was time off for the players, giving us the opportunity to recover, focus on our studies, and take some much-needed rest and relaxation from the rigorous college football schedule.

As we arrived at the Moshofsky Center, the team's indoor workout facility, Chip was waiting to greet us. He asked us to take a knee and then began: "I appreciate everything you guys have done for me, everything that we've accomplished as a team. It was all because of you guys. Everything I have ever asked you to do, you guys did it, and I will never forget that. But I have been offered an opportunity to go to the Philadelphia Eagles, and I'm going to accept that opportunity."

While it was shocking, we knew there had been talks. His name was hot among pro teams, especially after the past four successful seasons. He turned the University of Oregon into a national power while innovating the way the game of football is played. Chip was the real deal, and we knew he wasn't going to stick around Eugene forever.

"Down the line," he continued, "I promise I will never forget what you guys did for me. We've gone to battle together. So if I ever have the opportunity to look out for any of you guys down the road, I'm going to. What we were able to accomplish together was special."

As I sat on the field, I felt a sense of shock, sadness, and finality. It was clearly part of the coaching carousel. But Chip had done a lot for me. He pushed me harder than any coach had before, and his football genius was downright amazing. Mental toughness was at the core of his program. If you weren't mentally tough, you weren't going to be around for very long. He ingrained in us the type of lessons that stick with you after you're done playing the game: the reason football can be one of the greatest teachers in life. Every Saturday, at the end of our final team meeting before kickoff, he would have us stand up and repeat after him, as a team: *"Pressure . . . is what you feel . . . when you don't know what you're doing . . . but I don't feel pressure . . . because I know what I'm doing."*

Chip taught all of us a new way of life at Oregon. To win the day. It became our culture as a football program, and it became a core value for me as an individual. Knowing what you want is the easy part: anyone can think up a goal they want to accomplish.

The hard part is the process, the daily things you have to do to achieve those goals. And that applies to anything in life, not just football. If you take care of a single day at a time, without looking forward or back, you'll find yourself progressing as time goes on if you're willing to put in the work. Focusing on the process, one day at a time, is life-changing.

While I knew Chip was headed to bigger and better things, I also knew he left me with the lessons and tools I needed to become a successful man one day. Kelly told me the truth. He was one of the first people in my life that really held me accountable and told me the shit I needed to hear. By doing so, he helped me grow into a tougher person, and that toughness never left me. Kelly taught me that sometimes the truth hurts, but the truth needs to be said. You can't go roundabout; you have to tell the truth, and that's what he did for me. That's what he did for everyone on the team, whether you were a five-star recruit or the last guy on the bench. He told it like it was.

As a football player, you learn a lot from your head coaches. Instead of looking at the big picture, the end goals, I became process-oriented and detail-oriented by taking care of the little things before I even considered what happened next. If you take care of the little things, then the big things will take care of themselves. We were a top-five team in the country every year under his leadership, and he built Ducks football up from an average team to a real program, a national program, a national brand. And he did that by focusing on the little things.

For example, on weight room days, the team wore the exact same thing, even down to the smallest details like the color of our socks. We were expected to be five minutes early to every meeting and to show up prepared with a notebook so we could take notes about the things that would help us win that week. If you had academic or behavioral issues, you would pay. And if those things happened more than once, then your position group or potentially the whole team would pay. The uniforms were flashy, and the offensive scheme was fresh and new. Even so, Kelly had an old-school 1980s coaching style with very few pats on the back and "attaboys." We were always expected to perform to our standard, whether that was in the community, at practice, or on game day. We did that by doing the little things right and doing them often.

These lessons stayed with me and inspired my head coaching style. I often returned to Coach Kelly's guidance, in the good times and the bad.

When we broke out of that locker room to start the game, I knew something special was about to happen. You could just feel it in the air. We took the field with a purpose, a confident bunch of kids ready to play some ball. It was clear the community came out in full force. The scene was electric: the sounds of the home crowd, the smell of barbecue meats on the grill, and the bright lights of Friday night reflecting off our forest-green helmets.

As soon as we started the game, everything seemed to go just right. We won the coin toss and elected to receive the football first. Often the first drive of the game sets the tone, and this game was no different. Just a week before, on the first snap of the game, we couldn't even get lined up without a penalty. Now, with a new week and a fresh outlook, the Parkrose football team took the field with confidence.

After receiving the kickoff, our offense ran onto the field ready to get to business. Tre, playing in his second game of his life at QB, turned to me as he ran onto the field. "I got your back, Coach!"

I couldn't help but smile. "I got yours too!" I yelled back. "Let's go!"

From the very first snap of the game, my kids went after it. The first play, a handoff to the running back, Taydrian, went for an explosive twenty-five-yard gain. The next play, a QB keep for Tre, turned into another chunk of yards with the Parkrose community cheering as if we were in the Super Bowl. Two plays into the game Big Rick, Mile, and Kobe opened up holes in the defense big enough to drive a truck through. To cap off the first scoring drive of the game, Taydrian took the toss from the quarterback and bounced it out to the sideline with Polo as his lead blocker. The sideline full of players erupted as he broke free with no one in his path. *Touchdown Broncos!*

The kids came out with their minds made up. They weren't going to lie down. For the first time in ages, the student section had a reason to cheer. It was a wild ride. Touchdown after touchdown, big hit after big hit. Tre Singleton and Taydrian Jackson played like men on fire. The big boys up front created lanes and protected the players with the ball like their life depended on it. We scratched and clawed our way to a lopsided 50–0 lead in the first half alone.

I'd seen potential in these boys ever since the day I met them. The more I learned about their individual stories, the more I believed I was dealing with a special group of kids. But at the end of the day, my mission was to get them to believe in themselves. That Friday night was a special one.

We went into halftime, and it was like the game was over already. We put the backups in for the whole second half. They came in and picked up right where we left off. We ended up scoring 82 points and setting a school record for most points scored at Parkrose High School. I was proud, proud that my guys were finally able to turn the page on the past. I saw emotion, excitement, and passion. They celebrated each other's success and earned the right to call themselves winners by working together. The fans in the stands rushed the field to celebrate. It was amazing, like a big party on the 50-yard line. I stood there, surveying the crowd, watching our kids embrace, hug, take pictures with their classmates and family. They created this moment and they deserved to celebrate it.

We broke the twenty-four-game losing streak and did it in front of our families and friends. Just like Chip put me through the wringer and taught me so many valuable lessons on and off the field, I had done the same to these kids. That night's victory was proof that you get out what you put in. It might take some time. It might be hard. You might fall on your face. But eventually, if you continue to push forward, good things will happen to you. It came full circle right there for the guys. And that was a great feeling. To win. To succeed. To break the losing streak. Sure, it was just one game. But it meant everything to Parkrose. To these players. To me. Chip Kelly taught me that in football and in life you don't get what you deserve, you get what you earn. With their performance that evening, my kids earned it.

9

BUILDING STEAM

BE VALUABLE IN EVERYTHING YOU DO

We'd broken our losing streak , and it felt like the weight of the world had been lifted off our shoulders. For the first time in a long time, the kids at Parkrose won the day. But our work was hardly done. We were just getting warmed up, and I wasn't about to allow the team to celebrate for long. One win in twenty-five games is far away from a complete body of work. We broke the seal but still had a lot more to accomplish.

RJ, who was kicked off the team for his behavior in the preseason, continued to show up at practice and the games. I presumed he was done and would likely just throw in the towel and accept his punishment. However, to my surprise, during practices, with no direction from myself or the coaching staff, RJ chose to run on the track. He jogged lap after lap until he was blue in the face. When he was tired, he stopped and walked until he caught his breath, then jogged some more. It was impressive, to say the least. He was doing his best to prove he wanted to be a Bronco again.

During the first two games of the season, he stood in the front row of the student section with his jersey on. He wore his black Parkrose uniform proudly, regardless of the rocky start to his senior year. In my heart, I wanted him back, but I was cautious to avoid anything that would set our team back after they were finally figuring out how to be a team. RJ had dug himself a huge hole to climb out of. Nonetheless, I was proud to see his hunger to get back on the field.

On Monday, the start of the third week of the season, I approached him after practice to acknowledge his hard work. RJ, still sweating from two hours of running laps around the track, was on the edge of the grass field with his hands in the dirt. He was finishing up his daily workout with push-ups.

I walked toward him just as he was finishing up a set. "What's up, RJ? What's goin' on, man?"

He stood up in a rush as if he had done something wrong. "Hey, Coach . . . not much, just trying to stay in shape. How's everything going?"

"Not bad, RJ. I see you over here working. You've been going hard, it hasn't been unnoticed."

He paused. "Yeah . . . well . . . I was at the game Friday and saw what you guys did. I really want this, Coach. I really want to come back and be a part of this team. I'll do whatever it takes, Coach." He was sincere in his words, and his actions during the last two weeks matched. It was a lot to consider.

"Well, look, RJ, I appreciate all you are doing on the side. Like I said, everyone sees you over here working your ass off. And to be honest I really want to see you back on this team. But I don't want the old RJ back. I don't want the RJ that's going to bring people down with him. You can't do your own thing, you can't fight with coaches, and you damn sure can't throw your helmet across the field when you're pissed off."

I truly wanted to welcome him back with open arms, but my gut told me he needed another week of self-reflection. And in this instance, he needed one more good dose of the truth.

"For the sake of the team, I can't let you come back right now. I need to know you've changed first."

I stood there, looking at him. It was clear he was heartbroken. But this wasn't about football anymore. This was about life. I refused to let him get in his own way anymore, whether he agreed with my strategy or not. Even though I kicked RJ off the team in Fall Camp, he showed up every day and started running laps and doing push-ups on his own. But two weeks of punishment weren't enough. I needed him to look deeper within himself and understand that poor behavior and mistakes have real consequences. Small correctable mistakes we make as kids often turn into bigger, uncorrectable mistakes as adults.

I could see the frustration in his demeanor. His shoulders slouched, his head toward the ground. He was clearly deflated. "What do you mean? How will you know I've changed? I'm telling you right now I've learned my lesson, Lowe. This isn't fair!"

I calmly responded with a shrug. "Not everything in life is fair. This isn't up to me, RJ, this is up to you. You have to make that decision for yourself whether you want to be a part of this thing or not. We'll see."

High school sports can be an incredibly powerful teaching tool. You can kick a student out of the classroom, or send him to the principal's office, but most of the time, that student won't care. That sort of punishment will have little to no effect on him. Playing sports, though, is a privilege that has to be earned, making it the perfect area to teach a student that poor choices have consequences. If you kick a student out of practice, or hold them out of games, they might learn a lesson that will stick with them much longer. It hurts more when something you love to do gets taken away.

I watched as RJ dropped his head and walked out of the stadium. He wanted to argue with me, but by now he knew I wasn't budging. He kept his response short.

"Aight, I got you, Coach."

As he walked away with his chin to his chest, you could see the look of defeat on his face a mile away. I could only imagine the emotions he experienced. I was sure he felt the same anger and rage that had held him back in his young life. I was expecting a verbal assault from the young man, a disagreement that would ultimately show me how far away he was from understanding the point of all of this. However, I got the opposite. He probably hated me in that moment, but his response was calm and collected. That Monday afternoon was progress. The human side of me felt bad for the kid, but the coach in me knew I was doing the right thing. I was determined to help him change his life.

As our practices continued the week after our win, the energy and the juice in the room had shifted. The boys carried themselves with a different type of confidence after breaking the streak. Whether that confidence would last was still up in the air.

Our next game was against an unfamiliar foe, Hood River Valley High School. Hood River was a decently sized school with average sports programs. Their school was in a more rural setting than Parkrose High, just a thirty-minute drive down the beautiful Columbia gorge. When it came to sports, Hood River always had blue-collar kids that knew how to compete. They were a solid team that knew how to play physical and fundamental football. We were still learning those traits, but coming off a historic win, we could ride some positive momentum and give ourselves a shot to get another one under the Parkrose Friday night lights.

At Monday's and Tuesday's practice, we picked up where we left off. Kids were flying around and having fun; we were on the right track. It was special to see my boys reap the benefits of their hard work. My staff and I started to get into a rhythm as well. We had our set schedule of how we ran our program. It seemed to work well for us and our boys. On Monday after school we reviewed the Friday night game and made corrections with the boys on the things we needed to improve on. After our film session, we hit the field for a quick practice just in helmets. I took it easy on them on Monday, so we could get after it on Tuesday and Wednesday.

We liked to call Tuesday and Wednesday "workdays." We grinded on those days. We hit, we tackled, we ran, and we hit some more. The practice plan was part of our process, and the boys embraced it. On Thursdays, the day before the game, it was walk-through day. No pads, no helmets, just jerseys. This was the day we put our final touches on the week of work, while also allowing the boys a full day of rest and recovery before an intense game day.

After a successful Monday and Tuesday practice in preparation for Hood River, I felt like my guys were on the right path toward earning another victory. But on the Wednesday of the week leading to our third game, in good ol' Parkrose fashion we had to get out of our own way. My kids weren't perfect, and I knew that. All that being said, I still held my boys to a high standard.

Sometimes I understood their mess-ups, and other times I was dumbfounded and left scratching my head.

In the last half hour before practice, I was in my closet-like office, located in the old smelly locker room. I felt my phone buzzing in my pocket. I pulled it out and saw the name "Tre Singleton" on the caller ID. I swiftly answered the phone.

"What's up, Tre?" I figured he was somewhere in the school, maybe even on the other side of the wall inside the locker room getting ready for practice.

"Hey, Lowe . . . I might be a little late to practice today. That cool?"

I looked at the big digital clock on the wall. "How late are we talking? It's only three o'clock right now, you got about thirty minutes before practice starts. Everything alright?"

"Yeah, Coach, all good. I got an appointment right now. I think I'll be back a little bit after three thirty. I shouldn't be too late, just wanted to let you know."

That presented a problem. You can't exactly replace your quarterback. We couldn't even hold a practice without him. Our team had one quarterback and his name was Tre. With a team as small as ours, we didn't have many backups. On any given day, a player or two would pull an excuse out of his bag just so they could skip practice. Over the course of the summer and early parts of the season, I had heard them all. If a kid went through the trouble to make up an easily detectable lie just to avoid practice, I usually went along with it and hit them with a classic, "Alright buddy, see ya tomorrow then." But the handful of boys that seemingly loved ball never missed.

When my kids chose to skip practice or show up late, I could always make it work as long as I had one player—Tre Singleton.

He was the heart and soul of everything that we had going on. He was our only quarterback and best defensive player. On offense he made the plays, and on defense, from his middle linebacker position, he made the defensive calls. His story, his self-confidence, and the way he played the game left everyone inspired, me included.

On the phone I didn't feel the need to pry and ask questions. Tre was my guy, one of the few kids I could count on. He said he'd be "a little late" so I took his word for it.

"Okay, well, just hustle up," I said. "We're not going to start until you show up. We gotta get after it today. Most important day of the week! When do you think you're going to be done?"

"Yessir! I got you, Coach. Should only be about ten minutes late."

I hung up the phone, still thirty minutes away from our typical start time. As time started to tick away, I realized I'd made a mistake by not asking what the appointment was for. I sat in my office as the clock hit 3:30 P.M. The music from the locker room blared out of the speakers. My guys were loud and fired up for another practice.

The clock was moving, and before I knew it, the time read 4 P.M. Still no Tre in sight. By now the locker room was empty. The team had taken their party to the field.

My phone buzzed with a message from QB1: *Be there soon, Coach!*

We're not starting until you get here, I responded. *See you soon.*

Another thirty minutes painfully ticked away before there was any sign of Tre again. By 4:30 P.M., an entire hour after our scheduled start of practice, the juice and energy had left the team. The excitement and eagerness to practice was lost and I couldn't blame them. Half the team was sitting on the bleachers tired and depleted. The other half lay on the grass like they were being held for ransom.

After a full hour of playing the waiting game, a green Jeep Wrangler zoomed through the parking lot with Tre in the passenger seat. The car came to a screeching halt as Tre sprinted out of the front seat with his backpack over one shoulder.

Coming into this week, I could tell Tre felt pretty good about himself. He just won his first game of his high school career as a starting quarterback. On Monday, he was the big man on campus. His personality already placed him as one of the more popular kids at Parkrose. But after Friday night's victory, in his mind, he could do no wrong. That is, until his Wednesday appointment.

Now, to be fair, everyone has things come up in life. There are certain things that we all should get a pass: being sick or taking care of a serious personal matter. I didn't ask Tre what his appointment was for, but it had to be pretty damn important if he was going to be late to football practice, right?

As Tre jumped out of that car, and sprinted his way toward the football field, I noticed something different about him. Just a day ago, he had a head full of unkept, dark curly hair. As he ran frantically from the parking lot to the stadium, that messy head of hair was now a fresh fade. His lineup was crispy and his taper fade was on point. Then it hit me. That was his "appointment."

When you hear "appointment," a haircut isn't exactly the first thing that pops in your head. Here I was thinking he was taking care of something extremely personal. While we were here waiting, our QB was in the comfort of the barbershop chair. I was fuming.

I walked over and met him at the locker room door as he ran from the parking lot.

He yelled as he approached me standing at the entrance. "Sorry I'm late, Coach!"

After we worked so hard to get over the hump, we found a way to self-sabotage our success. If it wasn't one thing, it was another. I pulled him into my office and sat him down after instructing B-Jax to get the team warmed up and ready to go. I was furious.

"Tell me you didn't just make your teammates wait for you to get a damn haircut?! You told me you had an appointment, you think you're slick, huh?!"

By the look on his face, he knew he messed up. "I didn't think it would—"

"If we had anybody else, you wouldn't play at all this week for pulling a stunt like this. But we have nobody else. You've had every coach and player here sitting around waiting for you to get a damn haircut! You have got to be kidding me, Tre. That's selfish."

He hung his head as I continued to let him have it.

"I just lost all my trust in you," I said. "Now go get dressed, your teammates are outside waiting on you!"

My strategy for coaching this group of kids remained the same: love them up when they needed it, but at the same time hold them accountable for their actions. Tre wasn't a bad kid, and I know he didn't mean anything malicious by it. But at Parkrose, time and time again, it was one step forward and two steps back. I knew he cared by the look on his face. He knew he messed up, and the only thing to do when you make a mistake is move forward and do everything in your power to make sure that mistake doesn't happen again.

That day we managed to have a shortened practice. The hour delay evaporated any juice we originally had. Practice was sloppy, the boys were uninspired, and I wasn't my normal positive self. The day was a wash and we couldn't salvage it. The practices after a win are a test of how a team handles success, and we had failed. We limped our way to Friday night, hoping we could just get out of our own way. Tre eventually apologized and understood my expectation of him.

"Let's just put it behind us and go play ball," I told him.

The practice week turned out to be pretty shaky, but that didn't take anything away from the feeling on game day. Friday was upon us before we knew it. The players wore their jerseys to school with pride this week. It's amazing what one win did for the team. I was eager to find out what two wins would feel like. With a record of 1–1 we were exactly where we wanted to be. The battle with Hood River Valley High School would be an evenly matched game. The tougher team would come out on top.

The glow from the setting sun bounced off our forest-green helmets as we finished up pregame warm-ups and inched closer to kickoff. The game-day atmosphere never gets old, regardless if it's high school, college, or professional football. Each level has its set of unique characteristics that make it feel special. In professional football, you feel the history when you walk into the stadium. The Ring of Honor with names of former great franchise players and current Hall of Famers. College ball is about the fans, the tailgates, the students, and the ultimate pride that comes with supporting your team. The high school football atmosphere is different. It's more intimate, and feels more personal. This atmosphere is all about the community. One community versus the other, squared off on the 50-yard line every Friday night. For the second week in a row, the Parkrose community came out in full force. The grill was fired up, the band was rocking, and the student section showed up to show out.

During warm-ups, the refs called the head coaches to the middle of the field for introductions and rules explanations. It's more of a formality than anything else, and this Friday night was no different. I trotted to the middle of the field, shook hands with the six referees, and introduced myself. As I shook their hands one by one, the oldest ref of the bunch smirked at me.

"Hey, where's the head coach?" he said. "We want to talk to him."

It was a poor attempt at a backhanded joke. It annoyed the hell out of me. The tone of his voice was dripping with disrespect. His referee buddies let out a hardy laugh in support of his ill-timed joke.

I looked at them and kept my cool, doing my best not to be a smart-ass. "You're looking at him," I said.

Another ref doubled down. "You're the head coach?" he asked, pointing at me as if he couldn't believe it. "Aren't you a little young to be a head coach?"

I did my best to seem unflappable and confident faced with the referees' statements, but the passive-aggressive comments left my blood boiling inside. They knew what they were doing, and they knew I couldn't respond the way I would have liked to. After all, they were the ones in control of the game.

I held back my natural instinct to jab back and ask them what they were really trying to say. These six older gentlemen, none of whom looked like most of my football team, were trying to pick at me. I tried to stay levelheaded, intending to end the conversation and get back to business.

"I didn't know there was an age limit to be a head coach," I said. "You ready to play some football tonight or what?"

There were much bigger fish to fry than these subtle shots from the referees, but I left that conversation with a heightened sense of responsibility and protection for my boys. We were one of the most diverse schools in Oregon, and I was only one of two Black head football coaches in the state. At twenty-six, I was by far the youngest. This may have been the first, but I suspected it wouldn't be the last time I would be openly disrespected by referee crews that didn't look like us. The uphill battle continued to get steeper. There was always an obstacle around the corner, whether we brought it upon ourselves or not. I felt like a boxer on the ropes trying to keep my corner in the fight. Taking hit after hit, but refusing to give in. I loved these kids. Referees or no referees, it was time to go to battle with my boys.

Our kickoff team placed the ball on the tee and lined up for the first play of the game. Our sideline, full of players, began jumping up and down as the ref blew the whistle signaling the start of the football game. It was time to go to work. The crowd watching had clearly grown from the previous week, bringing an even greater energy to the old cracked stadium.

We got off to a blazing start. Our defense was up first. Coach Mike Garrity and B-Jax had the boys ready to play. We came out playing like our hair was on fire and quickly got the ball back for our offense. On our first offensive series, we drove it in for a touchdown and two-point conversion. Tre fed the ball to Jay Jay and Taydrian. Our running backs picked the Hood River defense apart. We picked up right where we left off, channeling the energy from our 82-point outburst last Friday night.

After another short series by our defense, we got the ball back and marched down the field to score another touchdown and complete another two-point conversion. *16–0, Broncos.*

We started fast and we were the more physical team. Big Rick and Mile opened running lanes for anyone who had the ball. Polo was a monster, shedding blocks and making tackles in the backfield. And our QB, Tre Singleton, showed command of the offense by leading our team down the field for two consecutive scoring drives. It reminded me of my Oregon Ducks days, where we would get in the end zone and hang 21 on the board before the other team had a chance to take a sip of water. Helluva way to start the game.

The opposing side had a tough team with tough kids, so they weren't going down without a fight. During the next Hood River possession, they lined up and caught their groove. They ran the ball over and over again, straight down the middle of our defense, until they finally scored a touchdown to cut the deficit in half, bringing the score to 16–7. We were putting together a good battle. We stalled on some drives but we stayed the course. After some back-and-forth defensive stops, Hood River got the ball back with 1:30 on the clock until halftime. One more stop, and we would take a one score lead into halftime.

With the length of the field in front of them, the Hood River quarterback threw the ball down the field to an open receiver on the sideline, who stepped out of bounds to stop the clock. Next play, the same result: a pass for a chunk of yards, then out of bounds to stop the clock again. The drive they were putting together was impressive. They managed to get to the 15-yard line with just five seconds left on the clock—time for one final play.

"Let's go, boys! They have to throw it in the end zone!" we shouted from the sideline. "One more stop!"

Our stadium was old and needed a face-lift. We had an old-school scoreboard to accompany the old-school bleachers, so when the clock hit zero on our scoreboard, a big air horn would sound off like in a basketball game. In most modern stadiums, there's no audio signal to notify the players on the field because if you start the play before the end of the quarter, the rules allow you to finish the play even if the clock hits zero.

Hood River snapped the football with five seconds left. The quarterback dropped back to pass and started scrambling around. He avoided one tackle, then broke another tackle from Kimball. As he avoided the pressure, the clock hit zero and the air horn went off, making an echoing *BRRRRT!!!* sound across the entire stadium and playing field. When the buzzer went off, Jay Jay, a basketball player as well, forgot that the play continues on and stopped as if the play were over. He was trained to associate a loud buzzer with a dead play. Unfortunately, we weren't playing basketball, but his instincts kicked in anyway, and he tragically stopped covering his receiver.

Just as Jay Jay stopped playing, the quarterback saw a wide-open receiver in the back of the end zone and launched the ball up for grabs. With no Bronco in sight, the receiver caught the ball in the end zone on the last play of the half . . . *Touchdown, Hood River.* You couldn't make this stuff up.

After a great first half, we walked into the locker room up by only two points: 16–14 instead of 16–7. In the locker room, you would have thought we were getting our asses kicked. Heads were down and tails were between legs. Everyone's demeanor was deflated. Jay Jay was embarrassed and the team was demoralized.

I did my best to rally.

"Fellas, we played a great half. Keep fighting! That was one play, flush it and move on. Keep your heads up! We can protect this lead, boys!"

My words fell on deaf ears. My team was down and out. We marched out of the huddle, warmed up for a few minutes, and then received the kick to start the second half.

On the very first play of the second half, I called a play that gave Jay Jay the ball, hoping to help him build his confidence back. Unfortunately, my brilliant plan backfired. Jay Jay ran downhill and took a light shot from the defense. Jay Jay went down, and stayed down while the trainers jogged out and peeled him from the grass.

We were winning the football game, but all of a sudden I could see us breaking down. Coach Garrity and I looked at each other on the sideline and nonverbally communicated, giving each other the "Uh-oh, we're in trouble" face. Jay Jay took himself out of the game. Shortly after the start of the second half, another player went down, and then all of a sudden, a third guy was down on the field. Big Rick, our defensive anchor, dropped a few plays later.

"Coach, I'm cramping. I can't go anymore," Ricky said.

I thought to myself, *This is going to be a long night.*

As the second half continued, the Parkrose Broncos dropped like flies. We were tapping out of the fight, and as a coach there's nothing you can do about it. We no longer wanted to play ball. The last play of the first half was so demoralizing that we tricked ourselves into thinking we weren't in this game anymore. I saw it all unfold in front of my eyes, and my hands felt like they were tied behind my back. All I could do was encourage them to keep pushing forward.

The kids quit on each other, and the kids quit on me. We

didn't score another point in the second half and ended up losing the game 16–23. Hood River came out in the second half and absolutely bullied us. What started out as a promising night turned into a nightmare of a performance. We put together a good first half against a quality opponent, but we couldn't pull through and battle through adversity like I had hoped. It was a heartbreaker because of the way our kids responded. It takes time to build mental toughness and it was clear we just weren't there yet. Although we'd taken them so far, we still had so much further to go.

The voice of Chip Kelly rang through my ears: "Whether you're up, whether you're down, whether you're a starter, whether you're a backup—you play your ass off every opportunity you get. If you're in one play or if you're in eighty plays, we expect your best effort. And if you don't play your ass off, then we're going to get somebody in that will."

The entire team knew we should have won that game. But we didn't. After letting ourselves down, we had some work to do. The kids were disappointed in themselves, which meant something to me. They all knew that they wanted out of that game, and needed to learn a simple lesson. If things go right or wrong, we never fold. We never quit. In life and in football, you never tap out of the fight. You fight all the way until the end. Although we were all disappointed in our performance and lack of resolve, we knew we were a family and we would live to fight another day.

The torturous weekend after a loss came and went. Once Monday came back around, I was ready to get back to the practice field with my guys. I arrived early to the office to prepare for practice the next day. I walked into the locker room, then my office, and shut the door so I could get the new game plan ready. As soon as the bell rang, all the players came into the locker room. I heard the boys through the closed door. They were never this early to practice, so I thought it was strange. They all came in, and I heard Polo's and Tre's voices.

"Aight! Quiet, quiet, quiet."

By the sounds of it they were having a player-only meeting. So, I put my pen down and listened from the other side of the door.

Tre spoke up first.

"I just wanted to have this meeting because I feel like RJ has served enough punishment for what he's done, and I feel like he's learned his lesson. He knows he messed up and we should give him another chance. I want him to come back on the team."

"I do too," Polo said. "I think RJ . . . he's learned his lesson. He's been through enough, and we wanted to vote to see if we all want him back on the team or not."

From the chatter and mumbling I could hear from the office, it sounded like they all came to a unanimous agreement that they wanted their friend back playing football with them.

"Well, what should we do? Should we not come out to practice and tell Coach Lowe we're not going on the field without RJ?"

"Let's all walk off the field after the warm-up!" another voice said. "That way we can make a statement and force Lowe to let him back on the team."

"No, we're not doing that!" Tre said. "That's a dumb idea. We have to practice, we have a game this week. And if we walk off the field . . . Coach Lowe will be pissed!"

The council agreed.

Tre stepped up as the voice of reason: "Well, why don't we just ask him? Let's tell him we want to meet with him before practice."

The team seemed to agree because another random voice blurted out, "Okay, you have to do it then."

"Alright," Tre agreed. "I'll text him, and see when he'll be here."

A few moments passed, and my phone pinged with a text from Tre: *Coach, do you have a second before practice? We want to talk to you.*

I was laughing to myself as I sent a text back and listened through the door for their response. Tre read my text out loud.

Yeah, I have a second right now. I'm in the office.

They all went silent and then I heard them start to whisper as they realized I was within earshot. "Wait what? NO WAY!"

I opened the door.

"So, you guys want to talk about something?" I said.

I looked from Tre's stunned face to Polo's and then scanned the rest of the huddled team members. I had to hold my breath to keep from laughing. They looked like they'd seen a ghost. They started freaking out.

"You were in there the whole time?!"

"I heard everything you guys said. If you guys want RJ back, then I will agree to it. He's served enough punishment and he seems to have learned his lesson, but we'll see."

The fact that these guys came together as a team made me proud. They went as far as to have an open forum so they could figure out a game plan together. That's what it's all about.

"If we as a family agree that we want him back, and that we can hold him accountable and help him through this, then let's do it. Let's get him back."

Bringing RJ back was like a shot in the arm. I remember pulling him aside after the next practice. He had just finished running yet another two hours of laps. I walked up to RJ, who was exhausted and covered in sweat.

"What's up, man? You doing alright?"

"Yeah, Coach . . . I'm okay," RJ said, still panting.

There wasn't much to say, and I wanted to make it short and sweet. "Your teammates talked. They want you back on the team." I could see his face turn from pure exhaustion to pure elation. "And I think you earned it. You showed us that you are dedicated to the team, and I think you learned a valuable lesson. Show up tomorrow ready to practice with your team."

The grin on his face spanned ear to ear.

"Thanks, Coach. I won't let you down! See you tomorrow."

After serving his suspension, RJ was finally back on the team. He knew what the expectations were and so did his teammates. It was finally time to give him a fresh start. He brought us much-needed energy, which I certainly welcomed. The kids were excited to have their buddy back, but with a record of 1–2 there was no time for a welcome-back party. We had to focus on our next game against Milwaukie High School.

RJ was early every day and stayed late every evening that week. I pulled him aside one day, feeling especially proud. "Whenever you're in the football game, you give me everything you've got." He played receiver like me, so I delivered an Oregon Ducks–esque message to him. "When we run the football, you need to block like your life depends on it. You need to protect your teammates when they have the ball. So when we run the football, you put someone on their butt, and you block like it means something to you." I was eager to see if my message had landed with the kid, and with the rest of the team.

The game against Milwaukie began in a relatively uneventful

manner. Lots of three and outs, few scoring opportunities, and tons of punts. Midway through the second quarter, we were tied. RJ was playing his butt off. Blocking. Catching. Running. Doing it all. He was still the same hard-nosed player I remembered, maybe even tougher. All that extra running clearly strengthened his mind.

We ran the football to his side early on. He did what his coach asked of him—put the player he was blocking square on his ass. It was a clean, hard-nosed football hit. Nothing to write home about, and certainly not a penalty. But getting blocked to the dirt isn't very fun if you're on the receiving end. And the Milwaukie kid took special offense to it. Just as quick as he hit the ground, he popped right up and retaliated after the whistle. He pulled RJ to the ground and began throwing punches. From the sideline I was thinking, *Oh no*. RJ was on the ground on his back, with the Milwaukie kid throwing haymakers to his face. Part of me wanted him to fight back, but I knew there'd be consequences if he did, even if he was clearly in the right.

The ref ran over to separate the two, and what I saw next was nothing short of amazing. RJ lying on his back with his hands up over his head, taking those licks right to the chin. This was the same RJ who threw a punch at a coach on the first day of summer workouts. The same kid who stepped to me with his chest out in the cafeteria after skipping workouts. The same one that had a meltdown in the middle of practice and threw his helmet across the field a week before our first game. The ref pulled the kid off RJ and took him to the opposite sideline. RJ hopped up, still with his hands above his head in the air, and ran to our sideline.

"Coach Lowe, Coach Lowe," he yelled. "I didn't swing back. I didn't do anything!"

"I know, man. I saw the whole thing. Great job!" I gave him a pat on the helmet. "Keep playing hard, kid!"

It was one of the proudest moments of my life. It almost brought tears to my eyes. I was so proud of him, and the rest of the team. Their growth and development was unreal. All the hard work paid off. Not in the sense of player performance, but in player development. RJ, and the rest of the team for that matter, were becoming young men. If we lost every single game left by fifty points, I couldn't have cared less. Nothing would take that moment of pride away from me.

Everyone on the sideline was cheering for RJ and patting him on the back. "Good shit, RJ! Good work!" The rest of the game, RJ went on to make big plays and helped us get our second win of the season, 21–14. And we won because of what RJ did. In many ways, he came full circle that night. We all knew what the old RJ would have done. But he had learned his lesson, and he finally re-alized that football is a privilege. It was a privilege he had to earn every single day by doing the right thing.

I was proud of his growth. I was proud that the game of foot-ball and tough love was able to rehabilitate his attitude and per-spective. While playing the game he loved, he ended up becoming a better person.

After that game, the Broncos hit a groove. Day by day, the boys continued to get better and better. We went on a three-game win streak, beating Rex Putnam High and Wilson High School by a combined score of 43–18. Our record was 4–2 and morale was high heading into the back end of our season.

The two weeks after our streak, though, had tough matchups as we faced a team from eastern Oregon and a private school. We lost those two games, but we battled and that's all a coach could ask for. Mental weakness was becoming less and less part of our DNA. Now, with a record of 4–4, we controlled our own destiny. If we won one more game, we'd make the state playoffs. It was amazing to even get to that point, from not winning a game in nearly three seasons to being a single win away from the playoffs.

We were matched up against St. Helens High School. It was a school about thirty-five minutes away from us. They had a solid program with a good coaching staff, but most importantly, they were in the same situation as us. We both sat at 4–4 with an opportunity to make the playoffs.

The Broncos were excited, and there was a buzz in the air. Leading up to the game, we put in a great week of preparation. Everyone was focused. Living in the moment. They were winning the day. St. Helens was similar to us in talent and positioning, but not in racial makeup. They were a mostly white high school, and there were a number of administrators in our school that warned me of racial tension between our two schools in the past. We would be traveling to St. Helens, so it was likely the referees wouldn't be very welcoming toward my group of kids. As coaches, we did our best to prepare our kids to potentially be treated unfairly, but to never stop.

"Don't make it about the refs or the other team. This is about you and only you," we continued to tell them.

St. Helens is a place where there aren't very many people that looked like our team, or that looked like me. In the past, race had become a problem between fans, parents, and players on the field. We refused to let that impact our game plan. We were going up to St. Helens to give it our best effort. Soon, it became clear that no one in that place wanted us to win, including the referees. I didn't want to believe it, but as the game unfolded, I'd see that race would become an issue once again.

From the opening kickoff, it was clear it was going to be a long night. The referees were one-sided and it was blatant. They'd call a penalty on us, but they wouldn't come over to me or my coaching staff to let us know what the penalty was for or what player it was on. They ignored our sideline the entire game. They called phantom penalties that no reasonable referee would flag.

We had the ball on the 5-yard line in the first quarter. After we ran the ball in for the first score of the game, I noticed a flag on the field. *Holding, Parkrose!* The touchdown was waived, and we were backed up. On the next two plays, they called two more consecutive penalties on us. We were on the 5, scored a touchdown, but ended up back at the 30-yard line after three nonsense penalties. It was blatant and it was disappointing, but we couldn't quit. We had to do everything we could to stay in the game.

I called the kids in. "You see . . . we talked about this. Control what you can control. That's all you can do. They're going to call what they want. Don't complain, just put your heads down and battle!"

Though the refs and the rest of the stadium were against us, the football gods were with us. We were up 7–0 when St. Helens got the ball and drove down to our 10-yard line. The St. Helens QB dropped back to pass and threw it up for grabs in the corner of the end zone. Desmond, a senior defensive back, picked the ball off, broke a tackle, and outraced the St. Helens offense for a 100-yard interception return for a touchdown. No flags. The refs couldn't do a thing. As the game continued, the hits seemed to get harder, and the refs weren't protecting our kids. Tre took a late hit out of bounds and got the wind knocked out of him. He got absolutely destroyed on the sideline, but limped back into the field of play. He's a warrior, but I could tell he was hurting. The risk of injury was especially dangerous because we didn't have a backup QB.

Tre started to run back into the game, but I stopped him.

"Catch your breath, Tre. Jay Jay! Go! You're at quarterback."

Jay Jay looked at me and gave me a head nod, indicating he was ready. Jay Jay lined up to take the snap. I called a zone read play that gave Jay Jay the choice to either keep the ball and run it or to hand it off to the running back. If you gave Jay Jay any space or daylight, he'd make you pay. That's the kind of athlete he was. He snapped the ball, read the defense, and made his decision. The defensive end crashed down the line of scrimmage, so Jay Jay pulled the ball and got loose.

The first defender thought he had him, but Jay Jay hit the brakes and watched him fly by. After the swing and miss, he side-stepped the next would-be tackler right before he capped off the run with a flip in the end zone. He was a magician with the ball in his hands, making the St. Helens kids look silly. That play turned the tides and we never looked back. The bad calls continued but our kids persevered. Parkrose, the lovable losers of Northeast Portland. Parkrose, the team who hadn't won a game in twenty-four tries. Just last year this team went 0–9 while being outscored 385–82. Everyone wrote them off, but they did it. With this victory, the once "Bad News Broncos" were now headed to the playoffs!

I saw Vice Principal Drake Shelton on the sideline and said, "I told you!" referring back to the moment when I told him I could turn the program around in a year. It seemed impossible back then, but we'd done it. Everyone was elated. The entire administration was at the game, watching their students accomplish something truly special. We had to battle so much over the course of that game. Despite the outside influences they couldn't control, my players put their heads down and kept fighting. We reached a turning point. A special moment where it was clear, now more than ever, that these kids were tough and had what it took to be winners. But not all roads lead to the promised land.

10

DAVID VERSUS GOLIATH

YOU CAN'T WIN 'EM ALL

Our reward for winning the play-in game was a date with Silverton High School, the number three seed in the region. This school was very talented, but we were excited to give them all we had. We were ready to take on whoever they put us against. We had to travel down to their part of the state, as we were the lower seed. It was an hour-and-a-half drive to a rural part of Oregon. The drive was filled with energy and confidence. The team knew it had a great challenge ahead, but it was ready and prepared to face it.

We drove into the town of Silverton in our school bus, and the whole town felt like a scene out of an old western movie. There was just one main road in and out of town flanked with old family-owned shops on either side. You wouldn't find a McDonald's or Walmart in this town. While our school wasn't particularly rich or wealthy, most of the kids lived in relatively populated parts of the state. They didn't have much small-town experience, and this was certainly new for them.

We quickly realized we were far from Northeast Portland, in more ways than one. As our team pulled up to the school, we noticed Silverton already on the field warming up for the game. They were running organized drills, and you could see from the parking lot that they embraced the image of the number three team in the state. They were twice our size. Most of the kids looked more like college athletes than members of a high school football team. Immediately, I sensed that we were the David to their Goliath. This wasn't going to be an easy game for us, even if we executed and played our best.

They were tough and they were huge, but the film showed they couldn't run very well. Our undersized team had no chance if we played the game between the trenches. Their sheer power and size would overwhelm us. However, if we could find a way to get out in space and use our speed, then we might have a shot. They didn't cover the edges as well as they did the inside of the field so outside it would be.

The team exited the bus and walked down to the locker room. I watched as they quietly put on their gear, clearly focused and ready for what lay ahead. Their quiet confidence was comforting. We had come so far as a team, and I knew we were ready for a battle. I couldn't help but think that we had a chance to win the game, because we had overcome so much together. If there was going to be an upset, it would be with this team. Parkrose was ready to deliver the performance of a lifetime on this cool November night.

Warm-ups were crisp and well executed. The kids were clearly engaged as they stretched, ran our usual pregame drills, and huddled up. I looked around at the team, taking a moment to absorb the electric playoff setting, and said to them, "This is our night! We didn't come all this way for nothing! Get out there. Play like we practiced and compete. Every snap, every play, every quarter . . . compete! Look them in their eyes and don't back down! Family on me, family on three. One. Two. Three. FAMILY!"

The boys broke out of the huddle, and it was time for the 5–4 Parkrose Broncos to face their next challenge—the 8–1 Silverton Foxes. In spite of what I thought was a strong pregame routine, the game started as badly as I could have imagined. On the first possession, Silverton pounded the ball right down our throats to take a 7–0 lead. They had us outmatched and outsized. This was precisely my fear. We just didn't have the line to compete with them. We were in trouble. The size differential was enormous, and we couldn't find an answer for it.

On our first possession, Tre took the snap and fumbled. Silverton recovered and had a short field to work with. Three plays later: *Touchdown, Foxes.* 14–0. It was starting to get ugly. We had to do something to stop the bleeding. It was time to pull out all the stops. After Jay Jay's performance last week, I worked all weekend to scheme up ways to get him in space so he could go to work. Those country boys were big and physical, but they hadn't seen anything like Jay Jay; he was special. I implemented a new package with Jay Jay at QB. We called it "Bronco." We had nothing to lose.

"Alright boys, let's go with Bronco. Jay Jay, cut it loose."

The guys were excited about it. Something new and fresh. A package of eight plays, all of them trick plays with Jay Jay at quarterback. A true game changer. We broke the huddle, Jay Jay at QB,

Tre at tight end, and big Polo at running back. The defense was confused, which was precisely the point. This wasn't the offense they'd studied all week.

"Ready . . . set . . . go!"

Jay Jay called for the ball as RJ ran toward him. Jay Jay faked the handoff to RJ and kept the ball with Polo as his lead blocker. If there was a player that could compete with Silverton's size and nastiness, it was Polo. Before you could blink, Jay Jay was running down the sideline with the country boys chasing him in slow motion. They didn't have a chance. *Touchdown, Parkrose!* A seventy-five-yard lightning-bolt run down the sideline. The Broncos were alive and well!

Our first touchdown immediately changed the attitude on the sideline. We went from down and out, fighting for air, to showing that same swagger that had carried us through the season. Hope is a remarkable thing, and we knew we could play with these boys.

Now down 14–7, our defense went to work. We took that momentum and got a stop on defense to get the ball back. Bronco package in the game. On the first play on the drive, RJ ran in motion toward Jay Jay before the snap. This time, we hiked the ball and handed it directly to RJ. He surveyed the field and took off. A forty-yard gain and a first down. On the next play, we handed the ball off to our big back Polo, and he burrowed forward for a ten-yard gain. We were rolling. On the third play of the drive, Jay Jay faked the handoff to Polo and kept the football for a quarterback sneak. With one man to beat on the edge, Jay Jay lowered his shoulder and delivered the blow.

WHACK!

You could hear it across the stadium. The defender's knees

buckled from the boom of Jay Jay's shoulders. With no one in front of him, Jay Jay high-stepped all the way to the end zone for another Bronco score, 14–14. We officially had a ball game.

Since our week-three meltdown, all we'd talked about was staying in the fight. And these boys stepped up to the call. They were no longer intimidated. They didn't give up. This was a new and improved Parkrose. One with some grit. Some attitude. The will to win. Jay Jay was finally playing to his potential and we could feel something special happening that night. After some back and forth, we got the ball again with the game still tied up 14–14. It was late in the second quarter, and we were backed up on our own 15-yard line.

In what seemed like a dream, Jay Jay snapped the football and put his foot in the ground to get vertical. He saw daylight, and with an athlete like him, that's all he needed. Dashing down the sideline, he made it past the first wave of defenders and was left with only the near-side safety to beat.

"Go, Jay Jay! Go!" we screamed from the sideline. Like lightning in a bottle, on the first play of the drive, Jay Jay Hudson took the ball eighty-five yards for a Parkrose Bronco touchdown. WOW! Jay Jay looked like a man among boys with his third touchdown of the half. Northeast Portland was outplaying and outracing the number three team in the state. Silverton had no answers for our speed.

Our sideline erupted when Jay Jay pranced into that end zone to give us the lead after twenty-one unanswered points. High-fives and chest-bumps were going around. If you were watching the game, you'd have no clue who was David and who was Goliath. We didn't just believe we were going to beat these guys; we knew it.

After Jay Jay scored, my boys were celebrating in the end zone. But that celebration was short-lived. Out of nowhere, a Silverton player ran up to Jay Jay and got in his face. I'm watching, helpless on the sideline, knowing I can't run out on the field to break it up. Only Jay Jay heard what was said, but whatever it was set him off. Within seconds of celebration, he clearly lost his mind. A shoving match commenced in the back of the end zone between Jay Jay and the player that hunted him down to talk some shit. Refs jumped in the middle to break up the scuffle between the two. Jay Jay was flailing his body around as one of the refs tried to break up the fight. A penalty flag flew in the air. They separated the two players, and both teams made it back to their respective sideline.

After the dust settled and the emotions of the situation calmed down, the refs huddled in the middle of the field to deliberate. A couple of excruciating minutes passed before they broke the huddle to come fill me in on what was going on. "Coach, there's fouls on both teams," the ref said. "Personal foul, taunting, on the defense and a personal foul, unnecessary roughness, on the offense."

"Got ya, we'll take care of it," I responded.

"There's another foul on the offense. Unnecessary roughness on the same player—making contact with an official. That player is ejected from the game."

I couldn't believe it.

"You have got to be kidding me!" I argued. "Your guy jumped in the middle of the two! You can't do this to my kids."

"Coach, I'm not going to argue with you, that's the rule," the official snapped back. "He's done."

During the scuffle, Jay Jay inadvertently made contact with the ref, a cardinal sin in football that gets you kicked out of the game. After an eighty-five-yard touchdown run and a bush-league taunting penalty by Silverton, our best player was done for the night. We were headed for the upset of the year, but it came crashing down just as we hit the halftime mark. It was a ticky-tack and soft call. The refs should have just let it go. There was no reason to influence the game like that when our player clearly wasn't the initial aggressor and was simply responding to whatever the Silverton player said. But, nonetheless, we were used to having these types of cards dealt to us.

From the beginning of most of these kids' lives, they often felt like the world was against them. I did my best to show them that the football field was the great equalizer, but there were still plenty of times when the scales were tipped against them. This might have been yet another one. But when you are always the underdog, you are used to scrapping for every inch. There was absolutely no way I was going to let these kids give up.

The half ended without any further excitement. In the locker room, our guys were down, and for once, I couldn't blame them. Admittedly, I was down too. Realistically, we didn't have a chance without Jay Jay, and in the back of my mind, I knew it was over. But it was my job to hold these guys together.

I never found out what that Silverton player said to set off Jay Jay, but I can imagine Jay Jay's reaction was justified under the circumstances. And though I couldn't prove whether or not he actually made contact with the ref, even though all my guys said he didn't, it didn't matter at that point. The damage was done and there was no sense in making excuses. We would have to play the second half without Jay Jay.

I did my best to inspire the team and keep them engaged in the game. The second half began, and we were a totally different

team. Frankly, it was no surprise. Silverton came out and domi-
nated the line of scrimmage, just like they did in the first two pos-
sessions of the game. My kids battled their asses off, but it didn't
translate to much success on the scoreboard. We just couldn't get
anything going on offense. Sack after sack. Incomplete pass after
incomplete pass. As deadly as we'd been with Jay Jay on the field,
we were back to being David. Nothing we tried worked. Sadly, we
lost the little advantage we had over Silverton.

Silverton took full control over the game, running the ball
down our throats. They gashed our defense for ten- and twenty-
yard gains every single time they handed the ball off. When we
stacked the box to try and stop the run, they'd toss the ball over
our heads for massive gains.

Despite our best efforts, we lost 50–26. Our season was over.

I could tell the kids were exhausted, devastated, and of course,
defeated. Sure, there was so much to celebrate, but it was natural
they were let down at the loss. Parkrose knew that if Jay Jay had
stayed in the game, the results might have turned out differently.

As we made it back to the locker room, I couldn't help but
look at these kids, battered and bruised, and feel a remarkable
sense of pride. I was proud that the players were pissed at losing. Not only did they expect to be in the game, *they expected to
win it.* How far they'd come! How much they'd grown! They
couldn't see it at the time, but our journey was a remarkable
one, and as they say, it's not so much about the destination but
the journey. We flipped the script on poor old Parkrose. With
a record of 5–5 and a playoff berth, we set the foundation we
long talked about.

The kids practically dragged themselves off the field. But, as we were walking off the field, I stopped the kids in the end zone. We took a knee, huddled up together, and I looked at the tears running down their faces. Every single one of them. Finally, they were living in the agony of defeat. You aren't sad when you lose if you go into the game expecting to lose.

This team was different. They expected to win. Hell, they demanded it. It was pure devastation, then, when they didn't. We stood in the end zone one last time as a family. Then, together, we walked into the locker room as one. As the kids settled in, I began to speak to them.

"Be proud of yourselves. You changed the culture, and we did what we set out to do. I love each and every one of you. And for the guys coming back next year . . . look around. Remember this feeling. Never forget this taste in your mouth. I know how you feel. What you're going through. The pain sucks, it really does. But it is temporary, it will eventually get easier."

I surveyed the room, and you could cut the disappointment with a knife. I felt it like they did. Loss was a hard pill to swallow, but I had been there and dealt with the agony of defeat.

It was 2014, and I was playing for the Oregon Ducks. We were a remarkably talented football team, led by future first-round NFL pick Marcus Mariota and an unstoppable running game behind Royce Freeman and Thomas Tyner. After a strong 11–1 regular season, we went on to crush the Arizona Wildcats in the Pac-12 title game for our twelfth win of the season. That pushed us into the first-ever College Football Playoff game where we were matched up against Jameis Winston, Dalvin Cook, Jalen Ramsey, and the Florida State Seminoles. The game took place on a beautiful New Year's Day in Pasadena, California. The Seminoles were on a historic twenty-nine-game winning streak, but even so, they were no match for our legendary Ducks team. They played a competitive game, but in the end we made quick work of them, winning 59–20 and solidifying our place in the National Championship Game against Coach Urban Meyer and the Ohio State Buckeyes.

This was our second-ever national title game appearance. I was on the team when we appeared in our first title game, in 2010. As a freshman, I stood on the sideline as I watched the Auburn Tigers' kicker make a game-winning field goal as time expired. It was heartbreaking, and I have never experienced such a painful defeat. That is, until 2014, when I was a starter. We entered the National Championship Game favored by almost a touchdown and loaded with talent.

But in the end the attrition of our thirteen-win season finally caught up with us. We hung tough in the first half but ultimately didn't have an answer for running back Ezekiel Elliott and quarterback Cardale Jones. The Buckeyes walked off the field that night as National Champions and all we could do was walk back to the locker room in defeat. My Oregon Ducks career had finally come to an end.

As I walked off the field, holding my helmet in my hands, I couldn't help but look back and watch the Buckeyes celebrating at midfield. The red and white confetti dropping down from the sky was gut-wrenching, and I envied their accomplishment. But football can be the highest of highs and lowest of lows. It can give so much and take so much away from you.

Thinking back to that moment, I knew what these kids, my kids, were feeling. I walked into the middle of the locker room, looked around at the thirty kids that had given it their all, and told them, "We will be back. I promise you; we will be back."

I was exhausted. It was a long day, both physically and emotionally. Looking back on the last eight months of my life, there was a lot to be proud of. But I was mostly excited for the next season. We very clearly exceeded expectations, as a school and as a team. Frankly, no one expected much of anything from us. After a twenty-four-game losing streak, how could they? But there we were, one half away from upsetting the third-ranked team in all of Oregon. Even though we fell short, there wasn't a fan in those stands that didn't clearly see that we had a chance to come out victorious that night.

Even though they thumped us in the end, we belonged. You couldn't persuade me that we weren't one of the top teams in the state. Our record may not have always shown it, but there was not a more battle-tested or grittier group of kids in Oregon. These kids came from nothing, had next to nothing, and were fighting battles most kids their age didn't have to think about. In spite of all of that, they showed up on the field day in and day out to compete. It was their escape, their sanctuary.

We started with nothing. Not even a properly lined and cut field. Over those eight months I played the role of a lawn mower, Uber driver, therapist, referee, and in between all of those, a coach. When it all came down to it, though, we found a way to be a team. This group of losers that no one wanted found a way to develop into a team that everyone cheered for. It was easy to get behind them. The swag, the personalities, the joy in succeeding.

As much as I probably taught them on the field, they reminded me of a lot of things I needed off the field. To dream. To never quit. To always be there for your boys. At the conclusion of that first season, it was unclear who the teacher really was. I came to Parkrose to reshape a program, and in doing so I think I rediscovered myself. But, even after all the lessons I learned during the season, the biggest one at Parkrose was yet to come.

11

AN ANGEL IN THE HALLWAY

LOVE IS THE ANTIDOTE TO HATE

The world works in mysterious ways. But even so, it always seems to balance itself out. Throughout the first twenty-six years of my life, I sensed that the world had given me so much. During the most challenging times, I always seemed to meet a person or fall back on a lesson that carried the day. I think back to the limited time I had with my father. He taught me amazing life lessons and instilled in me the confidence to tackle the world. Then there were the lessons football taught me. I was lucky enough to have great coaches in high school, college, and as a professional coach. And of course, I have been so fortunate in having a mother who worked hard and sacrificed so my siblings and I could have what we needed.

Each of these important figures set an example for how to help others. I firmly believe a higher spirit put them in my path to create and nurture my ability to serve. And even growing up, I intuitively knew I wanted to support those around me. I learned that through the struggles of my father. When he couldn't be there, I fell into the role of being the man of the house. My younger brother needed me to set an example and show him the path. In growing up quick and being there for him as a father figure, I likely learned more about myself than my brother did from me. This started my life of service, as I recognized just how rewarding it felt to help other people.

In looking for ways to help others, I found myself. For years, I thought football was my life. But my true calling was to be a positive, guiding force in the lives around me. And when I fully dedicated myself to making a difference, I started to feel wholly fulfilled. My heart was heavy with love and it became the most rewarding collective experience of my life. Now, more than ever, I know I was put on this earth to be here for others.

That drive for fulfillment was why I returned to Portland to coach. I wanted to see how I could be there for young people who may not otherwise have a role model. I took on the challenge that stood ahead at Parkrose High School. But eventually coaching football wasn't enough.

After our incredible first season and the excitement heading into my second season as the full-time coach at Parkrose, I sought more opportunities to get involved and be part of the culture at the high school. The main reason I took the coaching job was to help the kids, and I couldn't imagine sitting out the off-season. I became the head coach of the track team and also, with a steady push from Mr. Shelton, took on a third job as a security guard for the school. It offered me the opportunity to help so many more kids than just those on the football or track teams. Even then, I knew I still had a great debt to pay. The world had given me so much.

Before I got my "badge" to be an official security guard, I attended a mandatory district training program. Instructors taught us about how to handle several sensitive scenarios, including a live shooter. Of course, you never really think you are going to apply those lessons. That's usually the point where you mentally check out, thinking, *This will never happen to me.*

May 17, 2019, started like most other days. I woke up, grabbed an early workout at Parkrose, and ate a quick breakfast in my office before school began. During the school day, I was one of three school security guards. It was monotonous and uneventful for the most part, usually the most exciting experience being a silly schoolyard scuffle or an escort out of a classroom. But even then, I relished the opportunity to walk the halls and interact with the students. By the time spring rolled around, I had settled in to my new way of life. I understood the student body and enjoyed the extra time I got to spend with my football team during the day.

I always did my best to talk with the kids I passed in the hallways. We'd talk about sports, current events, or the newly released Nikes that all the kids coveted. It was just small talk, but I enjoyed it. Occasionally I'd see a student having a tough day, and I would pull them aside and see if they wanted to talk about it. The kids seemed to open up to me more—maybe because I was one of the younger staffers at the school. I wanted to bridge the disconnect that students sometimes feel from their teachers, coaches, and counselors. If kids have mentors and adults they trust and relate to, they are more likely to confide in them and share their feelings. When they do, we can begin to help them and prevent them from keeping things bottled up.

I was walking the halls that Friday in May like every other

day before. The bell rang, indicating the beginning of first period. Once the security guards cleared the hallway and ensured the kids made it to class, we would go back to our small, shared office adjacent to the cafeteria. It was nothing special: a few desks, computers, and a bunch of lost sweatshirts and school supplies.

The other two security guards at Parkrose were Coach Alves and an older woman named Mrs. Paula, but Coach Alves was off that day. It was just Mrs. Paula and me.

As we ran around taking care of our daily responsibilities, fourth period came around, indicating that Mrs. Paula would go on her daily lunch break. So, there I was, by myself, watching the clock tick through the day with my mind on our biggest track meet of the year in just a few hours.

Then, just before the noon school-wide lunch period, a call on the radio from the office came in: *"Security—can you escort Angel Granados-Diaz to the office from Mr. Meltzer's room in the FAB."*

It was the kind of call we got thirty times a day. *Security—do this; security—do that.* By now I was used to it. We were called to escort kids, break up fights, deliver detentions, take notes from the office to specific classrooms, and anything else in between. We were sent on blind missions, often not knowing what we were getting ourselves into because of the lack of information. We never knew *why* we were sent places, but that was the life of a Parkrose security guard.

The Parkrose building was divided into two parts. There was the main building, where 85 percent of the student body and classrooms were. The lobby, most classrooms, the gym, and the cafeteria were all a part of the main building. Then there was the fine arts building, also known as the FAB. In that building there were only four classrooms. The FAB was located about one hundred yards away from the main building, past the outdoor athletic fields and across a parking lot.

Once I got the call, I hopped up, grabbed my keys, and exited our small office. I headed through the corridor, hardly thinking about much of anything, just going through the motions of doing what I was asked to do. There could have been a million reasons why they wanted to see this particular kid, and most of them ranged from a quick check-in to something even more mundane. After reaching the building, I rustled through my oversized stack of keys attached to my belt until I found the right one.

I slid the key into the lock of the old building and turned it to the right. I heard the click as I pushed open that rusty steel door. It creaked open, as heavy as ever.

Parkrose was a dilapidated school, struggling to keep fresh coats of paint and even room numbers on the doors. It felt left behind in many ways, clearly in need of a great deal of maintenance. But that just wasn't in the budget. Even then, though, Parkrose had a great heart and spirit, the kind of energy you'd only get from a wonderful mix of cultures, identities, and personalities.

I entered the FAB building and walked into the cramped hallway with a bathroom immediately on my right-hand side a few steps from the doorway. The bathroom door slowly crept open. . . . I stepped forward, and almost immediately the bathroom door closed as quickly as it opened up. I glanced at the door, didn't see anything out of the ordinary, and kept walking.

I turned to my right and started to work my way down the hallway. I knocked on Mr. Meltzer's classroom and opened the door just enough to look inside. There was a substitute teacher at the head of the class.

I felt like I knew most of the kids in the school, but I wasn't familiar with the name Angel Diaz. I walked in and spoke to the substitute.

"Hello, sorry to interrupt, but I'm looking for Angel Diaz. Is he in class today?"

The substitute teacher glanced around, clearly looking for a little help from her class. The students surveyed the room and one of my players in a desk in the back spoke up.

"Nah, Coach, he's not here today."

I was in that classroom for about thirty seconds, just long enough to ask the question and get an answer. I stood five feet from the entrance when the door swung open. A figure in a black trench coat stood in the doorway.

The kid had black shaggy hair, glossy red eyes, and what seemed like a troubled look on his face. Something wasn't right. Within what felt like a split second, the kid motioned toward his trench coat, reaching inside as if to retrieve something. I didn't know it at the time, but the very kid I was sent to get was the same kid that stood in the doorway now.

The sunlight, shining bright through the frosted glass windows of the building, caught a large, dark-colored steel object. I saw the glistening reflection, still unsure what he had taken out. All hell broke out in the back of the classroom. It hit me—the black object he'd just pulled out of his coat was a shotgun.

Everything seemed to go into slow motion. Behind me were the sounds of kids screaming for their lives and desks smashing against the ground. And in front of me, a kid standing in the door-way of a classroom, with a shotgun.

The kids' screams were like something out of a movie. They were fleeing out the back door as if the room were on fire. I stood there with my feet cemented to the ground. Time slowed as I analyzed everything from the look in his eyes to the object in his hand. This was really happening.

The kid whipped the gun out of his coat. That's when my instincts took over. As he pulled the gun out, I rushed forward with both arms extended to grab the weapon. As I rushed forward, the kid flipped the gun in his own direction, pointing it at the middle of his stomach.

Everything was happening so fast. As I lunged toward him and just before I could get both hands on the gun, the kid pulled the trigger . . . *click*.

When I heard that click, I expected to hear a loud bang. To freeze in panic. For it to be followed by carnage and death. But instead, a miracle occurred. While the trigger clicked, the gun didn't go off. He only had time to pull the trigger once, as I was able to get both my hands on the weapon a fraction of a second after that fateful *click*.

I have heard a lot of different statistics, but everyone pretty much agrees that a single-barrel shotgun might jam once every 900 to 1,000 rounds. Meaning, for every time you pull the trigger, a shell will fail to discharge—the shotgun will not fire—only one time in a thousand. On that day, in that hallway, Angel had the universe looking over him.

I didn't stop moving. With my two hands on the gun, and both of his hands on the gun, we wrestled and banged into a file cabinet by the doorway. Kids were still screaming and rushing to get to safety. Once I got a grip on the weapon, I wasn't letting it go. We struggled to rip the gun away from each other while I consciously made sure to keep the barrel of the gun pointed toward the ceiling instead of at any of the students running out of the classroom, at me, or at the kid himself.

During the scuffle, our collective weight shifted around the doorway of the classroom and eventually into the hallway as I violently ripped the gun away from him. This fight, in what seemed like forever, lasted about sixty seconds. This was a different type of adrenaline rush than I'd ever felt before. My strength and senses were heightened to the maximum level.

After I took possession of the gun, I shouted for Mr. Hume, the teacher in the classroom next door, to come grab the gun out of my hand. I was holding the kid with one hand, talking him down, and holding the single-barrel shotgun in the other. Mr. Hume came and grabbed the gun, and it was in that moment I finally had the chance to look the boy right in the eyes. I expected to see the devil in those eyes. But I didn't. I saw quite the opposite. His pain, his suffering, his struggles were all so evident. He didn't need to be tackled, or beaten, or even held down to the ground in that moment.

This young man was crying for help. It wasn't in me to hurt him, even though most people in my shoes would have. No one would have blamed me for doing so either. I felt how scared he was, I felt his pain, I saw just another child crying out.

Instead of tackling him to the ground, I pulled him toward me. I hugged him to keep him close, to not let him run away. But I also hugged him so he felt seen, so he knew that even in a moment like this he wasn't alone. To give him a sign that someone was there for him, that I was on his side. This kid didn't need hurt, he needed love.

I told him I cared about him, that people cared about him. I could tell he was surprised to hear it. I wondered if he had ever heard that message before. It was like he was under a spell, and those words of love and care snapped him out of it.

He stood there in my arms, sobbing. "Nobody cares about me," he said. It broke my heart.

I squeezed him and said, "People care about you, buddy. I care about you."

"You do?" He looked confused.

"I do, bro," I said. "I just met you, and I care about you. Everything's going to be okay."

I felt an overwhelming sense of pain. Pain for how a child gets to the point of walking into a school, with a loaded shotgun, to attempt suicide in front of his classmates. I felt pain for how trapped he had to feel. How much suffering he must have endured. Those feelings still stay with me today. This was his call for help. His cry for support. He was living in a prison and couldn't find his way out. Death was better than life. It was the release he desperately needed. I pressed on with love:

"That's why I'm here. I'm here to save you. I got you, buddy."

I held him as tight as I could. Not because I wanted to prevent him from doing harm, but rather, because I wanted him to know someone loved him. He was in such a dark place in that moment, and frankly, he didn't want to hurt anyone but himself.

After I disarmed him, we sat there together in that quiet empty hallway before the police arrived. We sat there and talked for twenty minutes before a dozen cops barreled around the corner, SWAT gear on, guns drawn. That part scared me the most. They immediately pinned him facedown, snapping handcuffs around his wrists as I continued to console him. I understood the cops had to arrest him, but it was still tough to watch.

The cops took him out of the building and escorted me outside to a wild scene of yellow tape, SWAT cars, and news helicopters flying overhead. I saw Mr. Shelton there waiting for me. We looked at each other and both stopped dead in our tracks. Just feet away, I couldn't help myself.

I clapped my hand on my chest. "That's why you brought me here!" I'd just been in the most important fight of my life, and this was the man who'd brought me to this very moment.

After my work with the football team, I grew to love all the kids at Parkrose. I understood their struggles and what they were going through. In many ways, this young man in the hallway was similar to many of the kids on my Parkrose Broncos football team—fighting just to survive, while facing tons of challenges and obstacles in their paths. They fought, they battled, and day in and day out they defeated the odds. They had their good days but they also had their fair share of bad ones. That's part of growing up.

A lot of times, young people do things but don't really know what they're doing until they are dealing with the consequences. This is just one example of how far it can go. It's inevitable that young people are going to make mistakes. Some of those mistakes are big ones, like walking into a school with a loaded gun, and some can be smaller in nature, like bullying another kid or doing drugs and drinking alcohol. But the mistakes add up, and even one small mistake can have terrible consequences.

Identifying mistakes before they are made isn't always easy either—a lot of young adults are still in the process of learning the difference between right and wrong. Angel didn't fully understand what he was going through, the emotions and the pain. People deal with pain in different ways, and unfortunately this young man chose to attempt to take his own life. You never know what someone is going through.

Imagine how challenging it is for a young person to feel that nobody cares about them. Sometimes all it takes is one bad experience on top of that feeling, to push them to the point of no return. I can't say for sure if that's what happened with this young man, but it is a consistent narrative that occurs on a far too regular basis.

I didn't hesitate to help him that day because people never hesitated to help me. All it took were four simple words: *"I care about you."* Even today I think about how those four words saved our school. The struggling kid needed to know that someone, anyone, was there for him. He didn't want to hurt anyone, he just wanted to be seen, to be loved, to be appreciated. On that day, I was his angel in the hallway. The universe put me there to give him the lifeline he desperately needed. On that day, and in that moment, I learned that love can change the direction of our lives.

When the media learned of the incident, they flooded Parkrose and started live news feeds with commentary about an active shooter on campus. There were police cruisers, armed trucks, helicopters, and dozens of news vans. My phone started buzzing again and again, first with calls from my mother and sister to make sure I was okay. They didn't yet know what had happened. I stood there on the phone outside of the fine arts building and explained what I had just been through. With a shaky voice, clearly scared yet relieved, my mom said to me: *"That's the reason you're there. That's why you're at Parkrose."* Later on, when talking to a reporter, my mom said, "A lot of times we don't know why we are where we are, but everything happens for a reason. It's amazing all of it happened and his life leading up to it prepared him for that specific moment. He acted. Instinctually, he acted."

Her words rang true for me. As a lifelong athlete and football player, I always said I wanted to give back, to help people. And the world called on me. It was as if it had said, "Alright, Keanon, you say you want to change lives. You say you want to find a purpose. You say you want to be here for the kids. Well, prove it, right here, in this instant."

My younger brother, Trey, later said: "When the universe knocks, you've got to answer it. The universe is going to test you. You've got to answer those calls."

From that day forward the people in Portland called me a hero. I never looked at it like that. Even in hindsight, I wasn't a hero. I was just balancing the scales. God put me there to make a play. And I did. In football, they teach you that you're really only as good as your last play. I am proud of how I handled the suffering student in the hallway, but I don't think I am a hero. In fact, I feel strongly there is a much bigger conversation we need to have. Not about what I did, but about what caused Angel to feel the way he did.

We are living in a mental health crisis in America. I saw it that day in May in particular, but I also saw it that first day I met the football team. I saw it in the kids' faces—that they need help. This crisis is rampant, and it had found itself in our school system. Our youth were struggling in a tremendous way. It is so important to surround ourselves with people who care about us, who love us, and who move us in the right direction, something that sadly has gotten more and more difficult.

I wanted my kids at Parkrose to know that it's okay to need help. To feel sad. Their teachers, counselors, coaches, all of us were there to help them. We were on their team, and it is our greatest pleasure to go to bat for them. We aren't going to judge or tell them that they are crazy because they feel a certain way. It is important that we give life to those emotions and work through them together. No one wins when you get to the point of wanting to do harm to yourself or to others as a way to cry out. Even if we don't see them initially, we all have teammates everywhere we look.

I don't know what Angel's situation was, and it is not my place to offer commentary on his friends or family, but I know he needed help. I often wonder if there was something we could have done, including me, to stop him from attempting to take his own life at school. I have to believe we could have. Maybe I didn't have a conversation with him one day as we passed each other in the hallways because I was too busy or thinking about the game that night. Who knows? We are all in this together. We are all responsible when a young person acts out in this way. Sure, it is their decision. But every action and choice are the sum of their experiences that led someone to that point. As members of his school and community, we all failed him. We failed him because in the end he didn't know that others cared, and we failed him because he was able to purchase something that could so easily end his life. I got lucky and was in the right place at the right time. But had I not been, I believe he wouldn't be here today. That would have been a tragic loss.

There are so many lessons we can learn from kids like this. Angel was arrested and prosecuted but wasn't sentenced to prison. Instead, he ended up with a compassionate prosecutor and judge who sentenced him to a treatment-oriented program that would help to rehabilitate him and focus on his mental health issues. I feel great peace in that outcome. Tragedy was avoided at Parkrose High, but I am not confident things will line up like this again. There was a lot of luck, maybe even divine intervention, at play on that day. I am forever grateful for that. But, as I've learned on the football field, without serious work and actionable steps, we can't hope to do better.

May 17, 2019, is a day I will never forget. But I also choose to remember every single day leading up to it. In many ways, I realize that, at least in part, the scales were remarkably skewed in my favor before that day. The mentors, the family support, the coaches, the players, and of course, the love. For every experience I had that involved hate, I experienced dozens of other examples of love.

Those lessons and experiences gave me the tools to be there for that student in a way that others hadn't been there for him in the past. There is no playbook for handling an active shooter, even if you go through the mandatory training. You throw out the book when a kid comes to school armed with a gun. And even if there was a playbook, I am certain the words "Hug the shooter and tell him you care" wouldn't be in it.

But that is what I did. I took all my experiences, all the compassion, all the guidance, all the support I had in the past and channeled it into one child. I knew it worked for me, and it saved my life. Why couldn't it save his? Why couldn't love give this kid a new perspective on life? And thankfully it did.

There have been so many people in my life who taught me to lead with love, including my players at Parkrose. I learned valuable lessons from the students at that school. I noticed how they responded when I asked them questions and actually listened to their answers. When I took an interest in their challenges and struggles. When I offered them a compliment or some kind words. They felt heard, uplifted, and empowered to work through the obstacles. And in offering these small moments, I quickly realized it not only helped them, but it helped me as well. I learned that a gentle touch, caring words, or thoughtful guidance carried far more value and impact than punishment or force might otherwise have. It was almost like they knew. They knew I would need all that love and all those lessons. I'd bet they didn't know it would be like this, but they gave me the tools to make the play. To save a life. To make a difference for an entire community.

Those teachings remind me every single day that love is the antidote to hate. It extinguishes it. Love acts like the strongest armor you could ever imagine against threats and outside risks. It is impenetrable and stops hate dead in its tracks. You can't get past it. And in this day and age, we need all the armor and protection we can get. Just like a football player puts on his pads to protect his body, we all must arm ourselves with love to protect our hearts. The world is not always gentle, and it poses many challenges. Ones that we might not otherwise get through if we aren't prepared.

In coming back home to Portland, I took on the responsibility of giving back and trying to pay everything forward and balance the scales. That hug, that small yet powerful expression of love toward this kid in need, literally changed all of our lives. And on that day, in that moment, it felt like the world looked at me and said, *Alright Keanon, we're even. We're even.*

12

A RIDE TO REMEMBER

DON'T THROW THE DAYS AWAY

nstinct.

Guts.

Determination.

Resilience.

Grit.

Those are what separate the greatest football players from the first cuts. The game of football moves extraordinarily fast, sometimes at warp speed, and it is your instincts, the habits you form from the repetition, that inevitably lead you to make the play or fall short of greatness. In that classroom, with a shotgun, a black trench coat, and a kid staring me right in the face, my instincts took over. I didn't think. I reacted. I made the play. You can't plan for a moment like that, you either run away or jump into action. Much like football, life has a way of putting you in a spot to make the move.

While the days and weeks following the incident passed in a

blur, the summer allowed me to slow down and truly reflect on the moment. The media latched on to me. The night of the incident a man dressed in casual business attire came knocking on my door. He was a representative for ABC's *Good Morning America*. How this man got my address was baffling to me, but in the midst of the craziest day of my life, I agreed to go on the national program and tell my story. Local news vans and reporters showed up and parked outside my house for the next week or so, looking to be the first local outlet to score an interview. I was living in the twilight zone. Thousands of people from across the world reached out via social media calling me a hero. One day earlier, I was proudly walking the hallways of a forgotten school but now, twenty-four hours later, the whole world seemed to care about Parkrose. It was strange, but I understood the magnitude of the breaking news headline. Recent history will tell you that more often than not, a person that rushes a shooter in a school doesn't make it out alive to talk about it.

Every media outlet in the country, including *Good Morning America,* reported the incident with the same headline: "Football Coach Tackles School Gunman." On the television screen it sounded catchy, but I knew it was far from the truth. I did my best to articulate how the events took place, but without the release of the school security footage no one except me and Angel would know exactly what happened in the hallway that day. I was told by school officials that the video surveillance belonged to the Portland Police for their investigation and would never be released to the public.

We had three weeks left in school, and Vice Principal Drake Shelton decided it would be best to give me the remainder of the year off from working security. He recognized I needed some time to heal and decompress. The next few weeks were filled with messages from random people and calls from others I had crossed paths with earlier in life. It was as if I had passed away and yet was able to read and hear my eulogy. *He was brave; he's a hero; if there was anyone that would stop a shooter, it would be Keanon.* Life was surreal. As the dust settled I became more aware of just how special a situation the universe presented to me.

During those last three weeks of the school year, I still popped my head into school from time to time, but for the most part I kept to myself. Working security was a draining job, even without a moment like that. The life of a public-school security guard was much more than your average nine-to-five. Through the long days and the battles with students there was always an opportunity to make a difference in a young person's life. That is, in my opinion, the responsibility we all have: to teach and protect the younger generations growing up in this confusing world.

The incident sent a shock wave through the school and the community, and I was at the center of the detonation. The administration handled the aftermath of the situation well. They knew our kids needed a mental break too. It would take time to work through the emotions that were triggered by that day. During the lockdown, Parkrose students sat in those dark classrooms for hours, until the police units escorted them out to the safety zone. The whole experience was incredibly traumatic.

We took those last three weeks to heal as a school, and to ensure everyone was okay before we all broke away for summer. The administration focused on the mental health of the students instead of the usual end-of-year grind of final exams. It was a smart move by Drake Shelton and the other decision makers at Parkrose High School. They put the well-being of the students first, and it proved to be the right thing to do.

As the school year wound down, the media frenzy slowly calmed as well. After everything that had happened, I sat back and reflected on how proud I was to be part of this community. Nothing, however, made me prouder than watching RJ graduate that June. When we first met, he had been a kid with a bad rap and an even worse attitude. I saw the potential in him, taught him hard lessons through the game of football, and he ultimately ended up for the better. He trusted me as a leader, and I believed in him as a young man. The change was night and day. To get back on track and graduate, he had a long way to go. After the season ended, he put his head down, showed up, worked hard, and stopped making excuses. He walked at graduation with his classmates, and I couldn't have been prouder to be a small part in his life journey.

After the last week of school, my football team started year two of our summer workout program. We were coming off a successful season with most of our players returning. Aside from RJ, the whole crew was back: Jay Jay, Taydrian, Polo, and Tre, all hungry and ready to work. At the first summer workout meeting, there were more kids than I'd ever seen at any practice or informational session. After a season of bumps in the road, we had a shot to use the hard lessons we learned to do something really special.

In some ways, the school shooting showed these kids just how much I cared about them, and it confirmed that I wasn't just another coach preaching clichés. I really meant what I said. The first time I met these kids, I stood in an auditorium, looked them in the eyes, and told them from that moment on, we were family.

I would be there for my family when they needed me the most, regardless of the circumstance or situation.

Every kid in the entire school looked at me in a different light. Even the ones that didn't play ball. There were kids in that school that I had, for lack of a better term, beef with as a security guard: the kids skipping classes, the kids always getting in trouble, the kids that I had to battle with to get them where they were supposed to be. After that incident, every kid in that school, especially the troubled ones, respected me.

My team shifted their attitude to a full buy-in. If ever there was some hesitancy or conflict, that subsided after the incident with Angel. We had our summer workout meeting and hit the ground running. The team met regularly, trained together, and began to prepare our minds and our bodies for the next season. It was full dedication on everyone's part, and I was so proud of them. Something changed in them, just as something had changed in me.

Their response in year two reaffirmed that I was coaching these kids the right way. There had to be a balance between being tough on them when they needed it, while also understanding their life situations. I had to teach them the hard lessons, but also show enough love to encourage and build their confidence. Any good coach is always going to self-reflect and ask themselves the question, *Am I really walking the walk, or am I just telling these kids what I think they should hear?* I left the classroom with the shooter with tremendous confidence that I would do everything I said I would do. I care about the younger generation, and in a moment when my natural instincts took over, my heart led me to do the right thing.

As we began the next season, I added three more coaches, all former teammates that I played with during my time at the

University of Oregon. They were not only great guys, but tremendous football minds. When I first joined Parkrose, I had to beg to get a staff. Former high school friends and college teammates turned me down left and right. Going into that second season, and after making headlines, everyone wanted an opportunity to lend me a helping hand. My team felt wanted on that football field.

We couldn't wait for our first game. A new year with even more expectations. Right out the gate, we played our opening game against Prairie High School, the same team we opened with and lost to a year ago. Everyone in the area was excited to see what we could do after establishing our program in the first year.

It was a tough battle, but we lost our opening game again. We worked so hard and the confidence level was so high—maybe too high—that losing was a giant letdown. We followed up our disastrous performance with another loss in our second game and things started to feel pretty bleak. We'd felt invincible, and then all of a sudden, we're 0–2. But hey, that's football.

We hit our stride from there and rattled off three consecutive wins. This led up to a showdown against Pendleton High School, a big country team from eastern Oregon. A year ago, they smacked us up pretty good, scoring 41 to our 10. The matchup was set to be played in the small town of Pendleton, a four-hour bus ride away. Most people in the stadium didn't look like us; we were literally a long way from home. The game was epic, the small yet athletic Parkrose Broncos against one of the premier teams in the state. Our school had never beaten them before, but on that night our kids came to play. A legendary back-and-forth game turned out to be a legendary win for the kids from Parkrose. The Broncos had arrived. After the monumental win, I got back on the bus and rested my eyes for the four-hour trip back to Parkrose. All of a sudden, my phone started blowing up.

Obviously, I presumed friends and family were congratulating me about the big win. I figured they just got word about history being made out in eastern Oregon. I clicked on my social media, and it took a minute, but I quickly realized why my phone was buzzing nonstop with notifications. The media, almost five months after the incident, had just released the school surveillance footage from the hallway during the encounter with Angel. From my understanding, that footage was never supposed to come out to the public. The police, the school administration, and I were the only ones that had seen it up to that point.

The unofficial story had been that a high school football coach stopped a school shooter by tackling him to the ground. The video would now show the reality of what happened. It showed the moment me and Angel shared in that hallway. It didn't show an evil kid like everyone presumed. It showed a kid in need of love and a coach willing to see the humanity in him. The hug was something everyone could relate to.

The video aired everywhere: ABC, CNN, NBC, every major publication and news outlet again. It brought back a lot of emotion, but ultimately in its simplest form, it showed a child needing someone to help him in his moment of need and someone stepping up to answer that call.

The Parkrose Broncos won the next two games, leading up to a championship matchup against Wilsonville High School, a team we had never beaten in the history of the school. They regularly won our league and were a group of affluent kids from affluent neighborhoods. The complete opposite of our program. They had the best facilities, trainers, staff, and equipment. It was a stark contrast to what we were dealing with on our side of the tracks, but we had one thing they didn't have: warriors. My kids were on the verge of history, playing for the league championship against a powerhouse opponent on their field.

It was one of those storybook nights. One that almost didn't seem real. We pulled up to Wilsonville dead silent on our yellow bus. My boys were locked in and on a mission. We were on a magical run but knew it would take one more against an Oregon high school giant in order to solidify our place in history. An hour and a half before the game, we walked off the bus down a long cement path toward the visiting team's locker room. That path took us past the giant windows of the Wilsonville High School cafeteria. As we walked by we couldn't help but see what was going on inside. We saw streamers, balloons, cake, and trays of food covered with tinfoil. Dozens of mothers walked around with smiles on their faces as they set up and decorated their postgame league championship celebration. By now, my boys knew respect was earned and not given. And that night, we were on our mission to get our respect.

As we walked by those cafeteria windows, Tre turned to me with a grin and said, "They have no idea what's coming, Coach."

Everything we did that night, we did like champions. My boys took the field with a look of ultimate confidence. They knew they were winners, but for the first time in their lives they were playing for the opportunity to become champions.

I stood there on the sideline as I watched my Parkrose football team kick the ball off to start the game. I couldn't help but think about all the hours, the hardships, and the lessons we learned together over the past two years. We continued to defeat the odds. After two years of work, my Broncos fully understood what it meant to be a team. In any sport, a team that loves each other and believes in each other can accomplish anything. The Parkrose Broncos were the ultimate example of that.

The game started with defensive stops by both teams. It was a slugfest. Long gone were the days of begging these kids to simply "stay in the fight." They were gritty, hardened football players now.

That night we were there to outfight and out-tough them for as long as it took. Tre Singleton showed why he was one of the best players in the state. We were leading 7–3 with two minutes left on the clock until halftime. We were looking at 4th and 5 at our opponent's 40-yard line. I called a time-out to talk over the decision with my assistant coaches: we either play it safe, punt the ball, and try to go into halftime with a 7–3 lead, *or* we go for it and try to put more points on the board.

"Go for it, Coach!" Tre yelled as he jogged off the field for the time-out. "We got this, let's go score."

He was right. We didn't get to this point by playing scared. That entire year we played and coached with no fear of failure. Why stop now?

I looked at the call sheet and knew exactly where the ball was going. On 4th and 5, the Wilsonville defense would definitely be zeroed in on our two best offensive weapons, Jay Jay and Tay-drian. They were special with the ball in their hands so I figured that was the discussion on the opposite sideline. Tre, already having run for a touchdown on a QB keep earlier in the game, was also a weapon Wilsonville was going to try to take away. Well, in order to take our QB away, they had to stack the box. In my eyes, the play call was simple.

After the time-out, we took the field and lined up in our formation. It was an empty set with only the QB in the backfield. Jay

Jay and Taydrian lined up on opposite sides, one to the right and one to left. Just like I predicted, the box was stacked and all eyes were on Jay Jay and Taydrian. Our tight end, Lebron Roebeck, lined up slightly off the ball right next to our right tackle.

Tre hollered the cadence, "*Down . . . set . . . go!*" On the snap of the ball both inside linebackers blitzed and both safeties ran to Jay Jay and Taydrian to double-cover them. Untouched and un-seen, Lebron darted straight up the middle of the field behind the blitzing linebackers. He was wide open.

Like every coach does, we screamed and pointed helplessly from the sideline as Lebron popped wide open. "You got him! You got him!"

Tre caught the snap, saw the blitz barreling down on him, stood tall in the pocket, and delivered a strike to Lebron in the middle of the field. Our sideline and our crowd erupted. Lebron trotted forty yards untouched into the end zone. *Parkrose 14, Wilsonville 3.*

We went into halftime with the lead, but these boys weren't satisfied until the game was won. The second half started with another back-and-forth defensive struggle until we broke through on another fourth-down conversion. This time it was a pass out of the backfield to Taydrian Jackson on the 8-yard line. We took the lead 21–6 heading into the fourth quarter. One quarter away from making history.

The Wilsonville football program was a proud program. Historically they won our league championship most years and found themselves playing deep into the state playoffs year after year. They weren't going to lose quietly. We made a few mistakes and they did what any championship team does, they capitalized on them. They rallied behind their own quarterback and cut our lead down to 21–19 midway through the fourth.

We carried ourselves as a championship program in our own right. At times we had to learn those football lessons the hard way, but after two years of competitive commitment, we felt like we had seen it all.

At midfield, with three minutes left in the football game, we had the ball on 3rd and 8. We were still hanging on to the lead by a thread, 21–19. But if we didn't convert here, the momentum from Wilsonville would most likely carry them toward a late-game touchdown for the win.

Again, I called a time-out to get us in the right play. We needed eight yards or else we would be forced to punt. With the game on the line, one play came to mind. We had practiced it for months, but had yet to call it in a game. With the league championship on the line, there was no better moment than now.

We all stood there huddled up on that cold November Friday night. I turned to Jay Jay and asked, "You ready?"

He looked me in my eyes and gave me one definitive head nod. I called the play.

Tre lined up under center, Polo took the field and lined up at fullback in I formation, and Jay Jay lined up directly behind him as the tailback. Everything seemed to go silent as the referee blew the whistle and wound the play clock.

Tre lifted his foot to communicate to our receiver to motion in. Tre called for the ball, "Set . . . go!!!" On the snap of the football Tre reversed out and underhand-tossed the ball to Jay Jay as he sprinted toward the sideline with Polo as his lead blocker. By design, the defense pursued Jay Jay once they saw him get the pitch. Jay Jay was our most dangerous weapon, and once he got the ball, the defense would collapse on him.

After months of practicing this single play, we had it down to perfection. Jay Jay caught the ball and sold the play like he was going to run for the sideline. It looked like a regular toss play to the defense . . . that is, until it wasn't. After three good hard steps selling the run, Jay Jay, the quarterback turned playmaker, gripped the ball with his right hand and stepped back to throw. The receiver we sent in motion, a senior named Dale Scott, ran at the safety as if he was going to block him, then took off over the top toward the end zone.

Just after Jay Jay reached back and let the ball go, the defense smacked him in his chest, flattening him to the ground. While the ball was in the air, the world went into slow motion. We stood there on the sideline while the ball was in flight, watching, hoping, and praying.

Dale sprinted toward the ball in the air. If he was a step too slow or if Jay Jay let the ball go a half second later, then the play would have been dead. But on that night, and on that play, we were perfect. Dale caught the ball and ran into the end zone as our sideline went bananas. It was the biggest play in the biggest game of Parkrose history. That night the Parkrose Broncos defeated Wilsonville High School for the first time ever.

Just a little over a year before, this same group of young men hadn't won a single game, 0–23. Through a belief in themselves, and each other, they found themselves standing toe to toe with the Oregon high school football giants. The first league championship in the history of the school. For the first time in their lives, my boys were champions.

We followed that up with another special performance on

our home field, making history again by winning the first playoff game in Parkrose history. But unfortunately, all good things must come to an end. The Broncos fought and battled, but ultimately didn't come out victorious in the quarterfinals of the state playoffs. The ride was over, but the legendary season would live on forever.

When the video from the hallway dropped, I started to get substantial calls with big opportunities. Everyone from *Dr. Phil* to *The Ellen DeGeneres Show* wanted me to make an appearance and tell my story. I was always thankful for the opportunities, but most of the invitations just didn't feel right. Then ESPN reached out, wanting to know if I would be interested in having them out to Parkrose to film and create a piece that would be part of a *College GameDay* special. That offer felt right so I agreed to it. While I didn't know exactly what to expect, it was a remarkable experience for me and my team.

The day it aired, a flood of emotions came back to me. Even though it had been months since the incident, it felt like I was right there again in that hallway. There I sat, watching video of the play unfold. Breaking it down, dissecting it, understanding that it could have gone a million different ways.

In that moment, I reflected on the things I was most proud of in my life. I was on the top of the world playing at the University of Oregon, and then I was at the top of the world coaching in the NFL at twenty-four years old. It seemed like I had everything I could ever want right there in front of me, but fate intervened and just like that my best friend passed away. One day, I had everything and the next, it felt like I had nothing. My life was built on staying positive, but during those moments, the darkness set in. I returned home, unsure of who I was and where I would go. I trusted the universe, knowing it would guide me out of the darkness and into my purpose. I stayed the course and I'm proud of that.

Most people would have stayed in the coaching business, searching for opportunities in the NFL or a gig coaching college ball. But I knew that if I pursued those opportunities right then and there, I wouldn't have given myself a chance to heal.

As strong as we are as humans, we are simultaneously so fragile. I knew I needed to take a step back in order to move forward. I needed to trust my heart. I moved back to my hometown, spent time with my loved ones, worked unglamorous jobs, and all of that led me to a group of kids that needed someone to care about them. That group of kids, that team, that whole school, led me back to myself.

At the end of the day, I like coaching. I like working with young people, and I like football. But the opportunity to help young people is so much more rewarding than the wins and losses. I have come a long way since Parkrose. I left the school after the second season to take on another challenge. Fate intervened again, and the pandemic struck, locking down the entire country and canceling many high school football seasons from state to state. Again, I found myself back to working a part-time job, scraping by.

But one day, out of the blue, I received a call from a figure from my past who had always looked out for me. It was Coach Chip Kelly. Knowing the high school season was canceled and that I was out of work, he offered me a job. This time, it was an assistant coaching position at UCLA where he was the head coach. Chip came through for me again, allowing me to coach in his program while putting money in my pockets during a global pandemic.

I accepted the position and moved out to Los Angeles. He gave me an opportunity to return to the college ranks and I was grateful for that. After one season with Chip and the Bruins, I was offered a similar position at the University of Nebraska, where I sit today and put the finishing touches on this story. I know my life is much, much bigger than coaching football on Saturdays. Now, there's nothing wrong with that. All things considered though, I do think that coaching would be the easy way out. It would be comfortable to stay in the coaching business, but that's not really how I've done things in my life. The more impactful thing to do is to figure out a way to reach and help even more kids than I already have.

It goes back to instinct. To trusting your gut to lead you to the place you need to be. As complicated as life often is, there are few things that are as pure as our youth and the game of football. There is no evil there. Only grit, determination, sweat, and the highs of victory and the lows of defeat. The pain is only temporary, for you are always given another chance at redemption, often just a few days later.

As my story unfolds, and I recognize there is still much to do, I realize that it was my journey, my life, all the hardships, experiences, obstacles, and, of course, each and every day that put me in front of Angel in that moment. My father taught me to do things the right way, that you get out of it what you put into it. My dad, indirectly, taught me that just because someone is suffering, it doesn't make them a bad person. My mother taught me to find a way. With three kids at home, she worked extra jobs in order to move us across town and send me to a private school known for its legendary football program. She trusted me, she put her team first, and she sacrificed in order to give us a normal life. Coach Kelly taught me to respond to the call. He challenged me, and instead of giving up, I rose to the challenge. Following him to the 49ers, where I saw Colin Kaepernick take a knee, taught me about bravery and the strength it takes to defend your beliefs. And losing my best friend taught me that our lives are fragile and precious. As a young person you feel invincible, but everyone is fighting a personal battle that others don't see. And when tragedy strikes, it takes time to heal. You can't rush it; you must trust your heart in leading you back to peace.

Then, there are the lessons from my kids at Parkrose. The cards they were dealt and the toughness that was inside of them. Tre Singleton, fighting against the odds as a homeless teenager. Jay Jay Hudson, battling the urge to quit, playing not because he likes the game but playing because he wants to be there for his teammates. And RJ Artis, the journey of a kid that people gave up on. Fighting his own anger and growing into a young man right before my eyes.

Every one of these lessons helped me find the courage to make the world just a little bit more accepting, caring, and loving. If even one of those experiences took a different trajectory, I might not have turned that corner to find myself face-to-face with an armed student. Had my mother not raised, nurtured, and taught me to love others, I might have tried to tackle Angel, hurting him, myself, or any of the other nearby students. If I didn't have the life-changing experience with my students on the football team, I wouldn't have understood what our youth were experiencing on a daily basis. Fate guided me to that moment, and my entire life, each and every experience, prepared me for it. And I am forever thankful.

Angel taught me the greatest lesson life could teach—love, not hate, can conquer all.

ACKNOWLEDGMENTS

It took a great deal of support and love to write this book. From the beginning of my life, I have been fortunate enough to have remarkable mentors and family members who have shown me the way. I couldn't have accomplished any of this without them.

To my mom, Jennifer: you are the definition of stability and someone who always put family first. I love you and cannot thank you enough for helping to mold me into the man I am today.

To my dad, Kevin: thank you for never giving in and never giving up on yourself or your family. I wouldn't be who I am today without your attention, belief, and love in me, whether you knew it or not.

Thank you to my brother, Trey, and my sister, Alisa. You both walked through this journey with me and had my back through it all. I couldn't have done it without you.

Thanks to all my coaches that helped shape me along the way. To my high school coach Ken Potter, and my college coaches

Chip Kelly, Mark Helfrich, and Jimmy Radcliffe. Together, we all built something legendary. You all pushed me to be better than I could have been on my own.

Thank you to my friends and my teammates. To Taylor Martinek, Dom Forrest, Dylan Jackson, and Jordan Lewis: we sure did share an amazing ride together. Thank you for always supporting me and having my back. It's been a long journey with our group of friends with a lot of highs and a lot of lows. But we've stuck together through it all.

Thank you to my players, specifically Tre, RJ, Jay Jay, Taydrian, and Kimble. You all allowed me to grow with you and, whether you know it or not, taught me things that I did not know about myself. I learned more from all of you then you might have learned from me. Thank you for allowing me to share our stories and bring them to life through *Hometown Victory*.

Thank you to the University of Oregon: you opened my eyes to a different world and offered me a place to grow and mature during the time I spent there.

Thank you to Parkrose High School: the support from the community has never stopped, and it has been a special place to be and is where I want to continue to try to make a difference as I move to the next chapter of my life.

Thank you to Bryn Clark and Flatiron Books for believing in our story and helping me bring it to life.

Thanks to Sabrina Taitz and Eve Attermann at William Morris Endeavor: this book would never have come to life without your hard work and ability to find a great home for it.

To Justin Spizman: thank you for reaching out to me and inspiring me to tell my story. You have been a collaborator, coauthor, and writer. I am so proud of the story we told together.

And finally, to everyone that loves sports in general: thank you for picking up this book, for reading the stories and hopefully applying some of the lessons that I was able to include in these pages. This book is for everyone out there who's looking for inspiration or hope, everyone who's looking for purpose or for someone to believe in them—this book is for you. Share the stories in these pages, because they'll make the world a better place.

ABOUT THE AUTHORS

Keanon Lowe is a football coach and former Division I football player for the Oregon Ducks. He gained widespread media attention in May 2019 after disarming an active school shooter and embracing him until the police arrived. After playing as a wide receiver for half a decade, Lowe went to work in Philadelphia as an analyst for the Philadelphia Eagles and then as an offensive analyst for the San Francisco 49ers. He was the head coach for both football and track and field at Parkrose High School.

Justin Spizman is an award-winning and bestselling author, ghostwriter, and editor. He has worked on *We Rise* with Xiuhtezcatl Martinez, *Taking Your Team to the Top* with Ted Sundquist, and is the coauthor of *Don't Give Up . . . Don't Ever Give Up: The Inspiration of Jimmy V*. Justin currently lives in Atlanta, Georgia, with his wife, Jaime, their two beautiful daughters, Dani and Bella, and their rambunctious dog, Bodhi.